THE FORMATION OF THE FIRST GERMAN NATION-STATE, 1800–1871

Studies in European History

General Editor: Richard Overy
Editorial Consultants: John Breuilly
                       Roy Porter

PUBLISHED TITLES

Jeremy Black A Military Revolution? Military Change
  and European Society, 1550–1800
T. C. W. Blanning The French Revolution:
  Aristocrats versus Bourgeois?
John Breuilly The Formation of the First German
  Nation-State, 1800–1871
Peter Burke The Renaissance
Michael Dockrill The Cold War, 1945–1963
William Doyle The Ancien Regime
Geoffrey Ellis The Napoleonic Empire
Donald A. Filtzer The Khrushchev Era: De-Stalinism and the
  Limits of Reform in the USSR, 1953–1964
Mary Fulbrook The Two Germanies, 1945–1990
R. G. Geary European Labour Politics from 1900 to the
  Depression
Graeme Gill Stalinism
Henry Kamen Golden Age Spain
Richard Mackenney The City-State, 1500–1700: Republican Liberty
  in an Age of Princely Power
Andrew Porter European Imperialism, 1860–1914
Roy Porter The Enlightenment
Roger Price The Revolutions of 1848
James Retallack Germany in the Age of Kaiser Wilhelm II
Geoffrey Scarre Witchcraft and Magic in
  16th and 17th Century Europe
R. W. Scribner The German Reformation
Robert Service The Russian Revolution, 1900–1927, 2nd edition

FORTHCOMING

R. G. Bonney The Rise of European Absolutism
David Cesarani The Holocaust
Hugh Gough The Terror of the French Revolution
John Henry The Scientific Revolution
David Stevenson The First World War
Clive Trebilcock Problems in European Industrialisation
  1800–1930

THE FORMATION OF
THE FIRST GERMAN
NATION-STATE, 1800–1871

JOHN BREUILLY

Professor of Modern History,
University of Birmingham

First published in Great Britain 1996 by
MACMILLAN PRESS LTD
Houndmills, Basingstoke, Hampshire RG21 6XS
and London
Companies and representatives
throughout the world

A catalogue record for this book is available
from the British Library.

ISBN 0–333–52718–6

First published in the United States of America 1996 by
ST. MARTIN'S PRESS, INC.,
Scholarly and Reference Division,
175 Fifth Avenue,
New York, N.Y. 10010

ISBN 0–312–16029–1

Library of Congress Cataloging-in-Publication Data applied for

10   9   8   7   6   5   4   3   2   1
05   04   03   02   01   00   99   98   97   96

Printed in Malaysia

Contents

List of Maps

Note on References

References in the text within square brackets relate to items in the Bibliography, with page numbers in italics, for example [17: *34–7*].

Editor's Preface

The main purpose of this new series of Macmillan studies is to make available to teacher and student alike developments in a field of history that has become increasingly specialised with the sheer volume of new research and literature now produced. These studies are designed to present the state of the debate on important themes and episodes in European history since the sixteenth century, presented in a clear and critical way by someone who is closely concerned with the debate in question.

The studies are not intended to be read as extended bibliographical essays, though each will contain a detailed guide to further reading which will lead students and the general reader quickly to key publications. Each book carries its own interpretation and conclusions, while locating the discussion firmly in the centre of the current issues as historians see them. It is intended that the series will introduce students to historical approaches which are in some cases very new and which, in the normal course of things, would take many years to filter down into the textbooks and school histories. I hope it will demonstrate some of the excitement historians, like scientists, feel as they work away in the vanguard of their subject.

The format of the series conforms closely with that of the companion volumes of studies in economic and social history which has already established a major reputation since its inception in 1968. Both series have an important contribution to make in publicising what it is that historians are doing and in making history more open and accessible. It is vital for history to communicate if it is to survive.

R. J. OVERY

To the many friends made
during my time in
Manchester

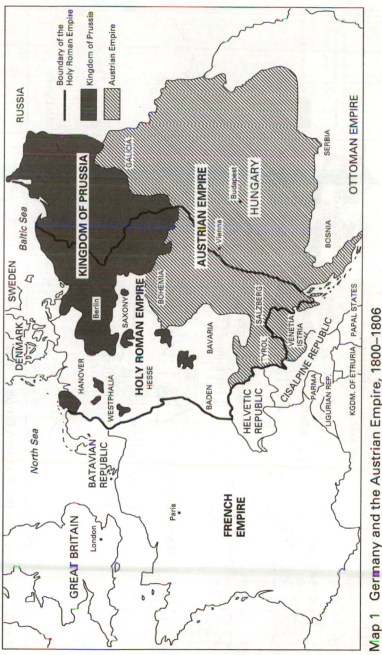

Map 1 Germany and the Austrian Empire, 1800–1806

Boundary of the
Holy Roman Empire

Kingdom of Prussia

Austrian Empire

RUSSIA

KINGDOM OF PRUSSIA

AUSTRIAN EMPIRE

HUNGARY

GALICIA

Budapest

Vienna

BOHEMIA

SALZBERG

SWEDEN

DENMARK

HANOVER

WESTPHALIA

Berlin

SAXONY

HOLY ROMAN EMPIRE

HESSE

BADEN

BAVARIA

TYROL

VENETIA

ISTRIA

CISALPINE REPUBLIC

PARMA

LIGURIAN REP.

KGDM. OF ETRURIA

PAPAL STATES

HELVETIC
REPUBLIC

BOSNIA

SERBIA

OTTOMAN EMPIRE

Baltic Sea

North Sea

GREAT BRITAIN

London

BATAVIAN
REPUBLIC

Paris

FRENCH
EMPIRE

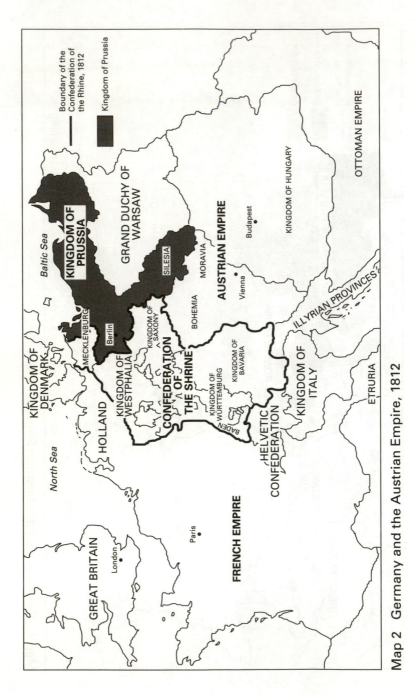

Map 2 Germany and the Austrian Empire, 1812

Legend:
Boundary of the Confederation of the Rhine, 1812
Kingdom of Prussia

Labels on map:
GREAT BRITAIN
London
North Sea
Baltic Sea
KINGDOM OF DENMARK
KINGDOM OF PRUSSIA
Berlin
MECKLENBURG
HOLLAND
KINGDOM OF WESTPHALIA
GRAND DUCHY OF WARSAW
KINGDOM OF SAXONY
CONFEDERATION OF THE SHRINE
SILESIA
BOHEMIA
MORAVIA
AUSTRIAN EMPIRE
Vienna
KINGDOM OF HUNGARY
Budapest
OTTOMAN EMPIRE
ILLYRIAN PROVINCES
KINGDOM OF BAVARIA
KINGDOM OF WÜRTTEMBURG
BADEN
HELVETIC CONFEDERATION
KINGDOM OF ITALY
ETRURIA
FRENCH EMPIRE
Paris

x

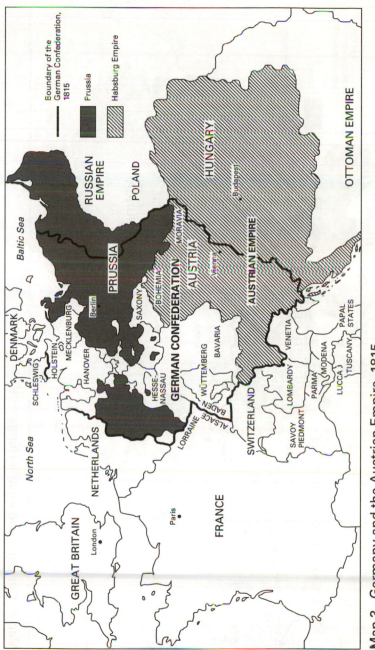

Map 3 Germany and the Austrian Empire, 1815

Legend:
Boundary of the German Confederation, 1815
Prussia
Habsburg Empire

GREAT BRITAIN

London

North Sea

NETHERLANDS

Baltic Sea

DENMARK

SCHLESWIG

HOLSTEIN

MECKLENBURG

HANOVER

Berlin

PRUSSIA

RUSSIAN EMPIRE

POLAND

SAXONY

HESSE-NASSAU

GERMAN CONFEDERATION

BOHEMIA

MORAVIA

AUSTRIA

Vienna

HUNGARY

Budapest

AUSTRIAN EMPIRE

WÜTTEMBERG

BAVARIA

BADEN

ALSACE

LORRAINE

FRANCE

Paris

SWITZERLAND

SAVOY

PIEDMONT

LOMBARDY

VENETIA

PARMA

MODENA

LUCCA

TUSCANY

PAPAL STATES

OTTOMAN EMPIRE

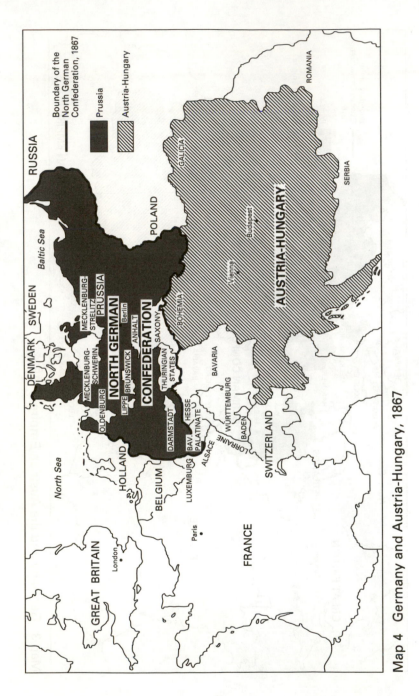

Map 4 Germany and Austria-Hungary, 1867

Boundary of the North German Confederation, 1867

Prussia

Austria-Hungary

RUSSIA

GREAT BRITAIN

London

North Sea

DENMARK

SWEDEN

Baltic Sea

HOLLAND

BELGIUM

LUXEMBURG

Paris

FRANCE

ALSACE

LORRAINE

SWITZERLAND

BADEN

WÜRTEMBURG

BAV. PALATINATE

HESSE DARMSTADT

OLDENBURG

LIPPE

BRUNSWICK

MECKLENBURG-SCHWERIN

MECKLENBURG-STRELITZ

PRUSSIA

Berlin

ANHALT

THURINGIAN STATES

SAXONY

NORTH GERMAN CONFEDERATION

BAVARIA

POLAND

BOHEMIA

Vienna

AUSTRIA-HUNGARY

Budapest

GALICIA

SERBIA

ROMANIA

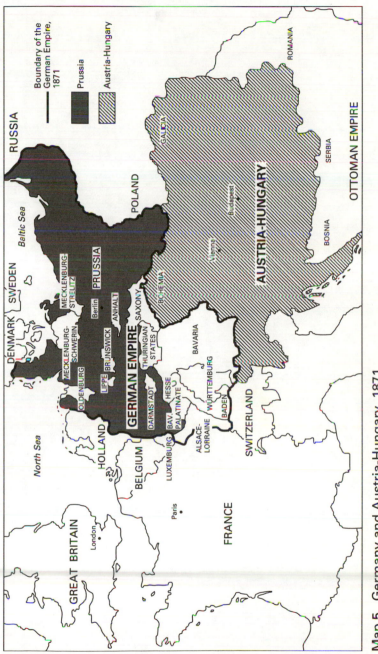

Map 5 Germany and Austria-Hungary, 1871

xiii

Introduction

The dominant note within Germany when the Second Empire was proclaimed at Versailles on 18 January 1871 was positive [2: *1–13*; 17: *34–7*]. There were critical voices of various kinds (see chapter 1) but the general sense was that this was a glorious and progressive achievement for Germany, as well as a major step towards the fashioning of a Europe made up of constitutional and national states in place of the reactionary forms of tiny states and multinational dynasties.

When that nation-state was finally and violently destroyed in 1945 the historical perspective was very different. For many Germans and non-Germans alike the nation-state, especially the German nation-state, supported by a vigorously nationalist population, was a threat to all civilised values. There was little protest against the *de facto* partition of Germany. The Federal Republic of Germany in its Basic Law of 1949 maintained the goal of national unity but always stressed that this had to take a 'western' form and must proceed peacefully, with the consent of other states and embedded within a range of supranational institutions [32: *193–265, esp. Preamble*].

Quite against all expectations, these goals were realised in 1989–90. Those who opposed such change raised the spectre of history repeating itself; those who supported it insisted on the fundamental differences between the new German state and its precursor of 1871. Yet in territorial terms the 1871 *Reich* established the general norm of what we understand 'Germany' to be once it had been stripped, after the First World War, of its Danish, Polish and French acquisitions. In 1871 that norm still had to be established [55].

We can now see the 1871 *Reich* as but one possible way of concentrating power into one or two centres in the German lands, one possible German nation-state – in terms of territory, institutions and legitimacy – and one of a range of nation-states. Furthermore, we know that nation-states can be unmade as well as made. Yet nation-

1

states are not accidental or arbitrary constructions; they are too pervasive a feature of modernity for that view to be credible. The major problem for historians of nation-state formation is to understand each case both as a matter of contingency as well as a part of a more general pattern of development. Each nation-state could have been different but the general pattern suggests that it would have been a different kind of nation-state, not an entirely different kind of state.

In this short introduction to the formation of the first German nation-state, the *Reich* of 1871, I will try to hold onto this tension between a sense of contingency and of necessity. My main concerns are to show that changes in the German lands could only occur in a particular European context; that there were pressures within the German lands which favoured the concentration of sovereignty into one or two centres; why, out of a range of possibilities, this reduction took the form of the exclusion of Austria from the rest of Germany and the formation of the Prusso-German empire of 1871;[1] and why the outcome was a nation-state.

I divide the book into four chapters: judgements of contemporaries and historians, conditions, processes and results of the formation of the *Reich* of 1871. The first chapter introduces the reader to debates which began at the time and have continued to this day. In the following three chapters I begin with the European context, move on to the German context, and then focus on Austria and Prussia. (Chapter 3 also considers the other two states involved in the wars of unification, Denmark and France.)

The European context – economic and cultural as well as political – matters in two ways. First, it shows us that nation-state formation was not confined to Germany and that the idea that the nation-state was the natural destination of political change was gaining more and more acceptance throughout Europe. Second, changes in the European balance of power have always been a necessary condition of major political change in Germany.

Germany was more than the two major states of Austria and Prussia. The policies and character of the other states – the 'third Germany' – placed important constraints upon the policies of Austria and Prussia. The modernisation of much of Germany before 1871 created the conditions in which political transformation in the German lands could be imagined and realised in the form of a German nation-state. In particular, the rise of a national movement throughout the German lands was of major significance.

2

The actual form in which the nation-state was realised in Germany conflicted with many of those imagined possibilities and various national ideals. It was ultimately a product of great power conflict, above all of wars, whose results were never inevitable. Therefore one has to study the states which went to war: their capacities, institutions, ethos, leadership, and diplomatic and military performances.

In chapter 2 I consider economic and cultural as well as political conditions. Chapter 3 on the processes of unification mainly focuses on war and politics and concludes by analysing the reasons for Prussian triumph. Chapter 4 considers the institutional arrangements and forms of legitimacy that accompanied the creation of the *Reich*. It also considers the possible alternatives to the actual formation of the 1871 *Reich* and asks what it means to describe the outcome as national unification.

I have not provided a general narrative. It is difficult to tell a story and pay proper attention to underlying conditions as well as considering what happened from a variety of perspectives. Normally the story is told from the perspective of its 'hero', usually Bismarck or, more impersonally, the Prussian state. There are numerous narratives of this kind and there is little point in adding another one. Instead, by focusing on the European, German, Austrian and Prussian perspectives, I hope to avoid some of the pitfalls of narrative history [54]. First, I include sections of analysis, considering conditions or outcomes of actions which were not necessarily acknowledged or foreseen by any of the actors. Second, I provide a variety of narratives in order that the reader can see how the story develops from the point of view of key actors in London, Paris, St Petersburg, Vienna, Copenhagen and the capitals of the smaller German states, rather than only from the point of view of Berlin.

I assume a basic knowledge of the major events. The maps at the beginning and the chronology, glossary, tables and bibliography at the end of the book are intended to help provide essential background knowledge.

Note

1. Attempts to provide short-hand characterisations of the *Reich* of 1871 are legion. Marx referred to the new state as the Prusso-German empire in his unpublished *Critique of the Gotha Programme* (1875), adding

a sarcastic and eclectic characterisation of it as a state which is nothing but 'military despotism cloaked in parliamentary forms with a feudal ingredient and at the same time influenced by the bourgeoisie, decked out by bureaucrats, and safeguarded by the police.' For the full passage see 120: *332* although I use the better translation of the quotation provided in 7: *30*. Henceforth in this book I will usually refer to this state as the 1871 *Reich*.

4

1 Historical Judgements

On 28 February 1866 Bismarck spoke to the Prussian Crown Council [223, 6: *611ff*; summary in 224, 3: *650–1*]. War with Austria seemed but a matter of time. Bismarck provided an historical background to the conflict, an interpretation which also justified the Prussian position. Ever since 1815, he argued, there had only been one healthy element within German politics: the Prussian state. Austria was a negative force, blocking change. She had consistently frustrated Prussian attempts to reshape Germany. The *Deutsche Bund* (Glossary; henceforth referred to as the *Bund*) which had been established in 1814–15 had not helped as its purpose was only to protect Germany against France. Prussia had had opportunities to act decisively, most notably in 1848, but these had not been taken. Now the time had come. Prussia must act to destroy Austro-Prussian dualism in Germany and with it the *Bund*.

Bismarck anticipated the work of the *kleindeutsch* (Glossary) school of historians who dominated the writing of German history between 1871 and 1918, especially the interpretation of how the 1871 *Reich* had come about [1: *90–123*]. However, these historians, unlike Bismarck, placed more emphasis upon the national and liberal elements involved in unification and less upon the dynastic struggle between Austria and Prussia. Their approach is made abundantly clear in the unfinished history of nineteenth-century Germany by Heinrich von Treitschke [3]. Chapters cut between accounts of German cultural development and the policies pursued by the Prussian state. The very structure of the book suggests a steady convergence between the two. The unification of Germany under Prussian auspices has an air of inevitability about it, a necessary fusion of power with culture, Hohenzollern tradition with German identity [see also 156].

It is easy to criticise this view. The *Reich* of 1871 was in many respects an accidental construct, the result of the fortunes of war, and was condemned by many contemporaries as a flawed and incomplete nation-state [2: *esp. 1–39*]. Furthermore, historical research since the end of the nineteenth century has gone on to consider many subjects von Treitschke barely mentioned – the growth of industrial capitalism, the social transformations induced by the rise of urban-industrial society and the cultural transformations which accompanied mass literacy and more effective communications [16; 18; 19].

Yet it remains much easier to criticise than to replace the Prussian perspective. Historical narrative is the telling of a story; stories are told in the light of the author knowing the ending. Very often the result of all this extra research and knowledge is simply the construction of a more comprehensive version of von Treitschke's story. Thus the battle over Austria's bid to enter the *Zollverein* (Glossary), a battle which Austria had lost by 1865, is sometimes seen as an economic Königgrätz [175]. Approaches which stress communications [105] or cultural associations [30; 179] or economic growth [18; 19] tend to fit into such interpretations in the same kind of way. When John Maynard Keynes adapted Bismarck's famous phrase about 'blood and iron' and asserted that Germany had really been unified by 'coal and iron', he simply shifted the perspective from Prussia's mission as a military power to that as an economic power.

Criticisms of the *Reich* as flawed or incomplete make normative claims. These critics usually desired a German state and considered this as probable, even inevitable, but did not find the actual *Reich* to their taste. Such critics often explained the outcome in ways similar to *kleindeutsch* historians but with the proviso that certain factors, such as Prussian military power, deformed this achievement. These critical voices point to alternative views of unification and alert us to the fact that the actual form taken by unification was but one of a range of imagined possibilities. That in turn can suggest different lines of interpretation.

First, and most vociferous, was the *großdeutsch* (Glossary) position. From this perspective the Austro-Prussian war of 1866 was a German civil war which resulted in the forcible exclusion of Austrian Germany from the rest of Germany. The new Germany turned its back upon many German traditions including the cultural pre-eminence of Vienna, the Catholic enlightenment of the late eighteenth century and the German presence in south-east Europe.

6

In the twentieth century this perspective has been developed by shifting the emphasis from states to peoples: the *gesamtdeutsch* (whole German) approach. The history of Germany is that of the German people rather than the German state(s). Such a history should include Austrian Germans [218; 185]. In a vulgarised racist form this argument justified the annexation of Austria and the Sudetenland to the Third *Reich* [63]. Understandably, there have been few proponents of the argument since 1945; indeed, if anything, Austria has been anxious to distance herself from Germany. Nevertheless, such a perspective reminds us that we must see Austria as a German power, try to understand her policies towards Germany up to 1871 in that light and ask how realistic and rational were such policies [199].

There is a perspective which extends beyond the *gesamtdeutsch* one. Austria was a European power with many non-German subjects. In 1849, as part of the process of restoring Habsburg authority and prestige, the idea was floated that the whole of the Habsburg Empire should join both the *Zollverein* and the *Bund*. This raised the spectre of a giant central European state. This *Mitteleuropa* (Glossary) idea was rejected in favour of the *kleindeutsch* national state but historians have argued that it reappeared later as an objective of German policy before and during both world wars [229; 82].

If we return to the national perspective, there is in addition to the Austrian and Prussian standpoints the view from the 'third Germany'. The other German states wished to avoid falling under the influence of either Austria or Prussia. They advocated forms of federalism which would weaken the authority of any central institutions. They tacked between the two powers, always trying to balance them against one another. However, in the unbalanced federalism of the *Reich* where Prussia was far larger than any other state, these federalist perspectives were marginalised and discredited, except in the work of a few historians, above all Schnabel [215]. Such perspectives have been revived since 1945 in the Federal Republic of Germany and have stimulated a more positive assessment of the German political institutions which preceded the *Reich*. The virtues and potential of the Holy Roman Empire [99; 100; 168] the *Bund* [187; 212], and even the Napoleonic Confederation of the Rhine [171] have been stressed. There has been research on the policies of various of the medium-sized German states [97].

This calls into question the idea that Prussian-led unification was

7

necessary for the achievement of vital national tasks such as the development of a strong economy and the provision of external security. Policies of economic integration and harmonisation and military coordination could have been pursued by means of federal arrangements. (In any case, demonstrating that the German lands 'needed' such policies is not the same as explaining why and how they got them.) It also draws attention to the fact that many Germans in important positions throughout the various German states who favoured moves towards greater national integration, envisaged this coming about in very different ways from how it actually did. However, research on the role of the 'third Germany' has also revealed that there were great differences between states linked to geography, confessional character and economic interests; that there were conflicting views of what state policy should be; and that powerful groups were often at odds with the policies pursued by their governments [97; 211; 212]. So the actual significance of these views and those who advocated them remains a matter of debate.

Also important is the role of nationalism in unification. In response to the positive view which sees national sentiment as supportive and possibly instrumental in bringing about the formation of the *Reich*, one can note two critical perspectives. One stresses that much of the national movement was opposed to the particular form taken by unification. The other argues that the national movement as a whole was unrepresentative of majority sentiment amongst Germans.

The first approach points to the radical and liberal features of nationalism. Nationalism began as a politics of opposition. For radical nationalists the idea of nationalism was one of popular sovereignty. To claim that the state should be national was to claim that all the members of the nation should play a part in the affairs of state. Radicals envisaged unification coming about as a result of popular political action and taking a democratic form, whether in a monarchy or a republic, though the republican idea was regarded as the most extreme form of radicalism in mid-century [150; 198]. Such radicals rejected the authoritarian institutions of the *Reich*, condemning it as a thinly disguised form of Prussian absolutism. Some, like Wilhelm Liebknecht, turned to the labour movement and socialism as the only way to create genuine democracy in Germany and thereby a real nation-state [78]. In turn the new *Reich* spurned the symbols of nationalism associated with radicalism (see below, pp. 111–12).

8

Many liberals eventually cooperated with Bismarck but both they and liberals who opposed Bismarck were critical of what had happened. The national state should be a constitutional state which provided uniform and equal rights to all its citizens. The failure of Prussia to liberalise her institutions before 1871; the grafting of imperial institutions on to Prussian and other state institutions; the illiberal features of those imperial institutions; the preservation of dynastic privileges and variegated state constitutions: all this offended liberals. However, they believed that history was on their side, that Bismarck would have to do what they wanted if he was to stay in power, and that the new state would move in the direction they desired. Only later did some conclude that they had been mistaken [170; 146: *123–40*; 197: *104–11*].

Such perspectives have been continued in various ways in more recent historical writing. Defenders of the Weimar republic sought to construct a liberal and/or radical tradition in which to ground their own position. Veit Valentin's great work on the revolutions of 1848, for example, brought out the strength and nature of the liberal position [220]. Erich Eyck's biography of Bismarck adopted a similar critical perspective although it was published much later [81]. The fragmentary works of Eckart Kehr sketched out a radical critique of the institutions and politics of the Second Empire. These historians, especially Kehr, were rejected and marginalised by the bulk of the historical profession [107 & 108; 185; 1: *ch. 8*].

A number of Kehr's essays have been collected, edited and published by Hans-Ulrich Wehler. Wehler and historians like him took up this critical perspective from the 1960s, consciously informing their historical work with democratic and liberal values. Explicit theory about the form a 'normal' developed nation-state should take has been used to buttress such a critical position. Unification has been seen as 'revolution from above', undertaken to avoid a more thorough-going 'revolution from below'. The consequent deficiencies in the Germany that was formed have been extended from the realms of political and military history to cultural, social and economic history [7]. In turn this approach has been attacked, for applying norms [203] or for applying the wrong norms [8].

The devotion of the German Democratic Republic (GDR) to marxist interpretations of history has considered unification as instrumental for the rapid development of industrial capitalism in Germany. Liberal nationalism, representing capitalist interests, combined with

Prussian power to create an authoritarian state which promoted those interests. In the later years of the GDR this interpretation acquired a positive element, including the treatment of Bismarck: capitalism was, after all, an advance on what had gone before [169; 183; 6].

These radical, liberal and marxist perspectives all imply that there was a widespread sense of national identity and desire for a German nation-state, even if the values associated with this desire were rejected, marginalised and sometimes repressed by the state which actually was created. They also imply that there were powerful social and economic interests pushing events towards unification. In this way their work can deepen rather than challenge the teleology of the *kleindeutsch* approach while being critical of the new state.

A more fundamental debunking of the national character of the new state argues that there was very little demand, certainly at popular level, for unification [31]. Germany by 1871 was still an economy dominated by agriculture; sentiments and identities were local or regional in character; the dynasties could still command considerable political loyalty; a broader sense of identity was as, if not more, likely to take a confessional rather than a national form. Indeed, the existence of the major divide between Catholics and Protestants in the German lands is increasingly recognised by many historians as of central importance in assessing the extent and nature of popular nationalism [151 & 152; 163]. What there was of a national movement was elitist, divided and politically weak and could make little positive contribution to the formation of the German state [31].

As these critical perspectives accumulate, so they erode the idea that national sentiments or movements played an important role in shaping the particular form of the German nation-state. They can be placed in a more general perspective which stresses the limited extent to which national identity had taken hold of the minds of most inhabitants of even France, let alone a country such as Italy [160, 74]. On the other hand, there are arguments which stress the extent to which, in Germany at least, a national movement and consciousness, even if regionalised and to an extent excluding most Catholics, was of vital importance in national unification [30; 201].

Scepticism about the significance of national sentiment or powerful national interests brings us full circle back to Bismarck, who constantly discussed the German problem in terms of the conflicting interests of the Austrian and Prussian states [200]. An interesting treatment of the subject from this perspective was *The Struggle for*

Supremacy in Germany by Heinrich Friedjung [4]. Friedjung, an Austrian German, took German nationality seriously and believed it played a vital role in shaping the politics of the German lands. However, that could have as easily led to Austrian as to Prussian supremacy in Germany, although such supremacy would not have assumed the form of a nation-state. The failure of Austria (as much as the success of Prussia) was one of leadership. Austria did not pursue a consistent policy either with or against Prussia. There were reasons for this (Austria's manifold international commitments, the growth of nationality conflict within the empire) but the inconsistency was not inevitable.

One could go further than Friedjung and analyse Austro-Prussian conflict with little regard to the issue of nationality. If that is the case, then it is the strengths and weaknesses of these conflicting states which should be at the centre of the historian's attention rather than issues such as a sense of national identity. Attention to the rapidly changing conditions of great power conflict would accentuate the contingency of the formation of the *Reich*. Something which was achieved in the period 1866–71, and even then hung in the balance, might be deemed highly unlikely to have had much chance of success just ten years earlier or later.

Thus we have moved from a perspective in which German unification took the only form possible which was prescribed by the fusion of nationality and power to one in which the nation-state was the chance product of clashes between major powers which could easily have ended differently.

It is not possible in this short book to subject each of these historical perspectives to a detailed critique. I have sketched them out briefly in order to convey something of the diversity of interpretation and complexity of debate over German unification. My own view is that both in Europe and in Germany there were strong pressures from the mid-1850s favouring the construction of large, modernising territorial states which made some provision for popular political participation and in which ideas concerning an identity between people and government were of increasing importance [33]. However, the *kleindeutsch* solution provided by an authoritarian and militarist Prussian state under the leadership of a unique political genius was just one possible, and perhaps improbable, outcome of such pressures.

11

2 Conditions

[i] Europe

[a] Economics

The period of German unification coincided with the high-water mark of economic liberalism in Europe. The pacemaker in this was Britain which had emerged from the Napoleonic wars as indisputably the greatest economic and political power in the world. Rapid economic growth – above all in the manufacture of textile and metal goods – had created important economic ties between Britain and Europe. Britain was dependent upon Europe for the supply of many raw materials and foodstuffs while Europe was a major market for British semi-finished and consumer manufactures. (This simplifies; Britain, for example, was a major exporter of coal to many coastal areas of northern Europe and imported many articles of manufacture from Europe.) The logic of this relationship eventually pushed Britain towards a policy of free trade, symbolised and most powerfully promoted with the repeal of the Corn Laws in 1846 and the Navigation Acts in 1849 [11: *ch. 1*].

Britain and other parts of Europe also looked to the rapid expansion of trade with the new world: west Africa, the newly independent states of Latin America and the vast potential of the United States of America. Trade in Europe shifted towards outlets on its northern and western coasts – above all at the estuaries of the Rhine, Weser and Elbe rivers and some of the Baltic ports. Germany was in the middle of such trade flows. For example, eastern Germany, along with other parts of eastern Europe, sent large amounts of grain to Britain and other parts of western Europe. Some of the earnings were spent directly on British manufactures but a good deal also on finished goods from other parts of Germany, especially the more advanced western regions. These regions in turn purchased many semi-finished goods from Britain such as pig iron for their growing industrial production. Such trade flows stimulated economic growth. The large deficit Britain ran with eastern Europe created a purchasing power there which stimulated the supply of needed goods in other European regions, and so on. This also makes it clear that one cannot treat Germany at this time as a 'national economy' [11: *ch. 6*; 182].

By the 1850s economic liberalism, if not a dogma, had become a conscious policy of many governments. By the early 1860s Belgium, Britain, France and the *Zollverein* had all negotiated liberal commercial treaties with each other and even the Habsburg Empire was tied into some of these agreements. With the shift of economic growth to railway building and the capital goods industries which that stimulated, contemporaries caught hold of an image of sustained economic growth based on modern, centralised forms of production and the increasing concentration of larger parts of the population into cities [174; 60]. Public opinion in Britain and France looked to those who aimed at constitutional government in large states and the pursuit of such liberal policies as agents of progress. By the same token conservatives in Europe took the view that maintenance of the international *status quo* and of a stable, agrarian society were closely tied together.

How far did relative economic performance suggest possible shifts in the relative strengths of the major European powers in ways which might favour the formation of a more powerful state in the German lands?

First, there is the demographic aspect to consider. In 1820 France had a population about three times that of Prussia and rather more than that of the territory of the future *Reich* (see Table I for this and what follows). By 1870 Prussia's population stood at less than half that of France, while that of the *Reich* was rather greater. Napoleon I could call upon the manpower of the largest European state (leaving aside Russia) at a time when manpower alone was the crucial condition of military strength; Napoleon III simply did not have such resources at his disposal.

But military strength has also, by mid-nineteenth century, to be linked to the nature of economic development. Russian population growth outstripped that of the German lands. However, Russia lagged behind in *per capita* economic growth and, above all, in the development of new methods of transportation and communication.

In the Napoleonic wars Russia could move troops as quickly as other European powers; they could fight as effectively; and they could be included in the occupation of Paris. By the time of the Crimean war steam-powered transport (ships more than rail) meant France and Britain could supply troops and material more quickly to the Crimea than Russia could.

British population growth matched that of the continent, as did her economic growth, and she remained well ahead as an industrial economy up to and beyond 1870. But British success had been coupled with a process of disengagement from European affairs. This combination of demographic and economic factors meant that in the period from the end of the Napoleonic wars to mid-century underlying conditions of military power had shifted against the western and eastern continental powers and in favour of the central powers. The balance of power between the central continental powers, Austria and Prussia, will be considered later.

[b] Culture

Liberalism and conservatism were much more than just political and economic doctrines but rather general sets of beliefs. In Britain and France and elsewhere in western Europe there was an increased emphasis on the need to have an educated population, to reduce the power and privileges of the churches and to stress enlightened self-interest as the basis for a stable and prosperous society. This liberalism derived from, expressed and promoted modernisation. The growth of communication beyond governmental control (commercial dealings, travel, associations, more extensive literary circulation) created the basis for a freer flow of information and the formation of public opinion. Liberalism in turn made a virtue out of these developments and, as an intellectual and political movement, pressed for the extension and institutionalisation of such freedoms.

At the heart of this liberal ideal was an assumption of underlying consensus based upon a common culture mediated through a common language. British and French liberals took for granted the idea of a national culture as the basis of political and economic freedom. One could only have constitutional government with a restricted role for coercion on the basis of such consensus. Such attitudes came to be especially important in France after the July revolution of 1830 and the coming to power of a regime which identified far more with Napoleon than with the restoration settlement of 1814–15. To a lesser extent it was also true of Whig-Liberal governments which came to power during the Reform crisis of 1831–2. Such values came to be part of the dominant consensus from the 1840s; the only significant issue being whether Britain should go beyond simply preaching the virtues of national liberalism and constitutionalism [113: *54–106*; 139: *Pt II, esp. 407–16*; 39; 154: *64–104*; 18: *135–221*].

There was a romantic sentiment in the educated public opinion which expressed support for national movements elsewhere in Europe. There was great British and French enthusiasm for the Polish, Greek, Hungarian and Italian national causes (rather less so for Germany), based partly upon the belief that these movements would favour reason and progress but also that they embodied noble, persecuted cultures. This sympathy was usually confined to nationalities that could lay claim to distinguished political and cultural achievements in the past and that dominated their regions, if not their states [68; 59; 42; 136: for English examples; 39: *215–23* for some general points].

Thus public opinion in western Europe tended to look sympathetically upon movements which could portray themselves as cultured, historical, civilised, national and liberal. Conversely there was much hostility to the Ottoman, Habsburg and Romanov empires which suppressed such movements. That is not to say that governments automatically pursued corresponding policies: frequently they did not. In any case it was often difficult to draw a clear policy conclusion from such sentiments, for example when defending the Ottoman Empire against the Russian Empire in the Crimean war. Nevertheless, these values formed an important backdrop to the formulation of policy towards national movements in central Europe.

Germany occupied a midway position in this regard. On the one hand, liberal German public opinion shared the broader enthusiasm for the Greek and Polish causes in the 1820s and 1830s [191; 193]. In 1848 German liberals (excluding Austrians) were initially supportive of the Magyar and Italian movements against Habsburg rule [114]. On the other hand, that same public opinion saw the German cause as a kindred one. Indeed, support for Greeks or Poles was, in part, a covert way of expressing support for the German cause under conditions of censorship and persecution. German liberals in turn looked to opinion in western Europe for support.

These were a very different set of assumptions from those made by conservatives, especially in eastern and central Europe. In these circles society was still seen ideally as being ordered by birth, privilege and Christian belief with the monarch at the pinnacle of this hierarchy, assisted by nobility and church in the maintenance of order. Conservatives such as the Gerlach brothers who played an important part in Prussian court circles in the 1850s regarded the populism of a Napoleon or a Gladstone with distaste. Orderly relations with subordinate groups were based upon the fulfilment of mutual obligations rooted in Christianity, not a shared secular culture. In many parts of Europe such a view of the world was under threat – from the impact of the French revolution, the reforms carried out in response, the commercialisation of agriculture and manufacturing. This, however, led to the development of a more explicit defence of that ordered world: implicit traditionalism turned into ideological conservatism. [For German references see: 80; 43; 103.] Such a conservative view had implications also for diplomacy and warfare. International relations were regarded as a matter of contacts between like-minded princes and their aristocratic servants who shared a common culture as well as familial ties. The prince remained commander-in-chief of an army which in turn was officered by nobles. Bismarck broke with many of these values politically but his reminiscences make clear just how basic and deep-seated was the assumption that German and European affairs were the concern of royal and noble families organised through the social medium of courts and that armies were animated by loyalty to their king and their religion. For example, Bismarck reflected on changes in the Russian nobility and the development of anti-German attitudes amongst the younger generation which he noted when ambassador in St Petersburg [226: *169–73; 227*, I: *241–3*]. Nevertheless, conservative assumptions largely worked in Berlin, Vienna and St Petersburg up to and beyond 1848, although they were faltering in the face of the growing appeal of nationality and constitutional government as the basis of political loyalty. They had little purchase in London and Paris. Importantly, however, such sentiments were more important amongst the elites concerned with foreign policy and they operated with a certain amount of autonomy from domestic political opinion [14: *ch. 12*].

Conservatism could come to terms with the idea of nationality. For conservatives this meant nationality understood as traditional and historical identity rather than as a commitment to popular sovereignty, equality before the law and constitutionalism. French conservatives had constructed a view of nationality which was critical of the revolution as a violent break with national traditions [119: 24–35]. The Bavarian Wittelsbach dynasty promoted the construction of national monuments after 1815 [54: *661*; 126]. The point about such conservative celebrations of nationality is that they did not contain disruptive political implications.

One should not counterpose these two sets of beliefs too sharply against one another. Liberalism in central Europe had aristocratic supporters such as Prince Leiningen and Count Szechenyi; bourgeois figures such as Schmerling and Bruck in Austria and von der Heydt in Prussia were loyal servants of their monarchs. Some political liberals were hostile to free trade; some free traders believed in authoritarian government. Nevertheless, much of the political conflict of the period was rooted in these different assumptions about how the world did and should work.

Radical movements also appealed to the idea of nationality. For every liberal nationalist such as Cavour or Szechenyi there was a radical equivalent like Mazzini or Kossuth. Gladstone enthused over the Italian cause and Garibaldi but so also did English radicals. The exiles of the Polish, Hungarian and Italian national movements who found refuge in Paris and London were divided between moderate liberals and radicals for whom national unity mean rule by the nation, i.e. radical democracy. (Generally for Britain see [35 & 164]; for responses to European nationalists see [42; 59; 68; 136]. For France see [134].)

The need to appeal to popular support within increasingly well-defined territorial states forced representatives of all political values to turn to the idea of nationality. The national idea received increasingly general currency across the political spectrum but equally was rendered politically indeterminate by virtue of its universal appeal. Broadly, as one moved from west to east the idea of nationality clashed more obviously with the political and social *status quo* and was the concern of an ever-smaller minority. For such a minority the nation was something to be made. Germany occupied a middle position: Germans did not live in a national state such as France or Britain but equally the cultivation of German national consciousness was not something that encountered repression from above and indifference and incomprehension from below. Germans were never

17

placed in a position of subordination to other language groups. It was not their national culture which was questioned so much as the attempt to organise politically along national lines [154; 57: *chs 4 & 5*; 83: *passim*].

[c] Power

The peace settlement made at the Congress of Vienna in 1814–15 has sometimes been criticised as anti-national. Those who pleaded for national political organisation did so in vain – whether in Germany or Italy. However, such advocates were few and lacking in power. The major problems the statesmen at Vienna had to address were rather to do with satisfying the interests of the major powers and deciding just how much of the Napoleonic transformation of Europe to undo [129; 12: *ch. 12*].

In territorial terms Napoleon's achievement was confirmed rather than undone. His simplification of the hundreds of states of Germany and Italy into tens of states was preserved and many native princes who had profited from this continued to rule over their new creations. Catholic temporal power was confined to the Papal States and the Catholic church had to find other ways of wielding influence than by means of state power and landed wealth.

Each of the victorious allies had to receive something for its trouble. Russia advanced in eastern Europe, above all in areas of Polish settlement. Prussia was thereby forced out of many of her former Polish possessions and took compensation in Germany. Austria secured territory in northern Italy and south-eastern Europe, did not seek to regain Flanders, and devised various methods of indirectly controlling other parts of southern Europe and Germany. Britain had little interest in European territory (though she did insist on the restoration of the state of Hannover which had the same ruler as Britain until 1837) but more in European security achieved through balancing continental powers against each other. Her major gain came with the destruction of the French global challenge. Britain and Austria also resisted an over-harsh treatment of France (although the 100 Days of Napoleon made this more difficult in 1815 than it had been in 1814) because they did not wish to shift from an unbalanced Europe in which France was too powerful to an equally unbalanced Europe in which she was too weak.

The general consequence was that Britain – the greatest econ-

18

omic power in the world – moved to a non-interventionist policy in Europe, seeking at best indirect methods of control. Her principal concerns were with a resurgence of French power and the containment of Russian expansionism. This had a peculiar effect, turning Britain into a defender of the Ottoman Empire and a reluctant supporter of national movements backed by France, and therefore creating some tension between public opinion and foreign policy.

France focused most of her attention upon European affairs after 1815, having decisively lost the colonial conflict with Britain. After 1815 she appeared potentially disruptive, especially in support of national movements.

Russia had emerged from the Napoleonic wars as the dominant land power; her armies which had swept westwards to occupy Paris were by far the largest of all the states involved. Within western and central Europe she appeared as the principal defender of the restoration settlement. However, in the Far East she had expansionist ambitions which could lead to conflict with Britain and in the Near East her concern to weaken Ottoman power was to bring Britain and France into an alliance against her.

The peace settlement was also designed to replace war with diplomacy by instituting a series of congresses as a means of coping with international disputes. The congresses, based on the idea of a common interest in the maintenance of legitimate states, soon ceased to meet but the strong pressures in favour of running down large and expensive armies meant that diplomacy continued to prevail over war as a means of settling international disputes in Europe. (By this I mean disputes between the major states. Those states had few scruples about military intervention in the affairs of minor states.) Until 1854 there was no war between any of the major European powers.

For a brief moment in 1848 this settlement appeared to be in danger. A major flaw in liberal assumptions was revealed: the changes liberals desired seemed incompatible with the maintenance of the 1814–15 settlement and yet it was that settlement which secured peace, the foundation of most other liberal achievements. In the event the French Second Republic did not seriously challenge the 1814 settlement, Habsburg authority was restored in her core territories, Hungary (with Russian assistance) and northern Italy, and the *Bund* was reinstated in 1851.

It was the Crimean war which finally undermined the Vienna

settlement. Britain and Russia, allies in 1813–15, went to war and Britain did so in alliance with France, the enemy of 1815. In turn the war forced Austria to adopt policies which offended her former ally, Russia. The era of alliances amongst conservative states to defend each other against national and radical challenges was over. The breakdown of settled alliances also meant that states could find themselves isolated in conflicts with a stronger state. This was to happen to Austria in 1859 and 1866 and to France in 1870–1 [13: *chs 6 & 9*; 21: *Pt I*].

— Arguably the Anglo-French effort in 1854–6 had a conservative aim: the preservation of the Ottoman Empire against Russian expansionism. However, it also created a basis from which the French ruler, Louis-Napoleon, could pursue more radical policies. Napoleon III was, in the eyes of many European conservatives, a suspect figure as he lacked proper dynastic legitimacy and his power was based in part upon appeals to the memory of his uncle and upon practices such as plebiscites and the manipulation of public opinion [119: *ch. 5*; 165].

The first result of a more radical policy came in 1859 with the alliance between France and Piedmont. The outcome was war with Austria, Austrian defeat, and then – for fear of provoking further problems – the rapid acceptance by Austria of independence for Lombardy. The construction of a north Italian kingdom under the Piedmontese dynasty, the House of Savoy, rapidly led on to the formation of a new Italian state embracing the whole of the peninsula and Sicily. France gained through the acquisition of influence in Italy, which replaced that of Austria, and the cession of Nice and Savoy by Italy [91: *ch. 9*; 21: *Pt II*].

One clear result was a substantial weakening of Austria. A second result was that the events of 1859–60 could be regarded as a model for those wishing to form nation-states elsewhere. It could also be taken as a warning. The new Italian state was clearly indebted to France and very much under her influence, having to provide material proof of her gratitude through the cession of 'Italian' territory to France.

By 1860 the territorial and institutional elements of the 1814–15 settlement were breaking down. There was an ominous aspect to this: states were resorting to war rather than diplomacy to achieve their goals. This led governments into programmes of military expansion and reform, both responding to and promoting further changes in the nature of warfare. In the Crimean war the use of steam power, in this case in ships, meant that British and French troops were better supplied than their Russian opponents. The Bessemer process provided the basis for reliable high-quality steel manufacture which helped transform both naval and land artillery. The Minié bullet, using a rifled barrel, gave rifles greater range and accuracy. The British and the French shifted to new forms of standardised gun production which both increased output and made it easier to introduce new weapons [123: ch. 7].

In 1859 both Napoleon and Franz Joseph were shocked by the devastation wrought by new weaponry at the battle of Magenta. France's victory was in part based upon her ability to use new methods of transportation and communication to mobilise and concentrate large numbers of soldiers more quickly than had hitherto been possible. Military reformers had to take account of these new possibilities. At first only limited lessons were drawn from this. Sometimes they were mistaken ones. For example, the Austrian infantry used rifles but inefficiently and were then beaten by French columns which engaged them in close combat. The Austrians then shifted the emphasis to shock charges on the enemy rather than improving their firing drill and rifles. The experience helped both Austria and many others to underestimate Prussia [28: ch. 1].

[ii] Germany

[a] Economics

At the end of the Napoleonic wars the economies of Germany – that is, the lands of the *Bund* – were dominated by agriculture. Some 60–70 per cent of the population lived by working the land, although this varied regionally. Broadly speaking, agriculture declined in importance as one moved from east to west, although it remained dominant in some western regions such as Bavaria and Hannover. Only in some regions – the Rhinelands, Saxony – was agriculture in second place behind manufacturing. Even then, much of this manufacturing was in light consumer goods, especially textiles, decentralised and rural [52; 11; 109].

This pattern did not apparently change much up to mid-century. There was considerable population growth (Table I) throughout

21

Germany but the overall proportions of the labour force in agricultural and non-agricultural occupations remained fairly constant. Only from the 1850s did the agricultural labour force decline as a proportion of the whole labour force (Table 1).

However, patterns of agriculture changed markedly. The Napoleonic period introduced or hastened such reforms as an end to collective forms of farming (strip farming, substantial use of common lands); shared property rights; the payment of dues or labour services to privileged landholders; the restriction of the ownership of manors to noble families [11: *387–96*; 16: *ch. 8*; 43: *ch. 8*; 66: *74–99*]. The result was a much more individualised and market-oriented type of farming, essential if population growth was to be sustained. Farmers who exported their products to other regions were interested in improvements in transportation and commercial liberalisation. Traditional forms of authority were difficult to sustain when the old nobility owned only a minority of manors and many of the peasant farmers now operated independently. The countryside was ceasing to be a conservative bastion of old-style monarchical, aristocratic and church authority [43: *ch. 9*; 16: *747–63*; 36: *ch. 2*].

Up to mid-century the major non-agrarian forms of economic growth mainly involved the production of consumer goods. There was some new-style industrial production but much growth was achieved by more intensified and commercial forms of traditional production. This in turn put pressure on traditional ways of organising manufacturing such as guild and urban monopolies [88: 37; 152: 22–37].

From the 1840s there was a marked shift in the forms of manufacturing growth. The railway boom channelled a good deal of people's savings from traditional investments such as land and bonds. It in turn stimulated the production of coal (for the smelting of iron ore and for steam power), iron and other capital goods. It also had the effect of promoting further regional specialisation. The fastest growing sectors of the industrial economy now involved larger firms, more capital investment in technology, and were linked to the growth of new urban centres. (In addition to general economic histories such as [11] and [125] see the account in [221: *589–640*] which places great emphasis upon the shift in economic development from around 1840.)

All this increased economic interdependence but also intensified economic conflict. When the *Zollverein* had been established in 1834 its major purpose, especially for the non-Prussian members, had been

22

fiscal rather than political or economic. The *Zollverein* had little national economic or political importance until the 1850s brought with it these new patterns of economic growth. Individual governments could not now lightly contemplate withdrawal from the *Zollverein*, not only because of their own financial concerns but also because they were likely to encounter opposition from within their own populations if they did so. In this way the emergent economic power of entrepreneurs constrained the freedom of action of German governments [92; 172; 188; 181].

At the same time there developed new conflicts between those economic interests which wanted the *Zollverein* to increase its trading with the outside world by means of tariff reductions and those who wished to protect branches of the economy against external competition. Both sides increasingly used nationalist arguments to buttress their case. The free trade arguments were especially associated with the naturalised Prussian John Prince Smith and the protectionist arguments of the so-called 'national economists' with Friedrich List [75; 93].

These matters acquired importance within the *Zollverein* from 1849. First, there was the attempt by Austria to bring the whole of the Habsburg Empire into the *Zollverein*. This was rebuffed by Prussia which in part used a low tariff policy as a way of excluding Austria, many of whose industries could not yet compete in the international economy. In 1851 Prussia pushed this policy further when she negotiated the entry of Hannover into the *Zollverein*. This in turn set the conditions for the renewal of the *Zollverein* treaty for a further twelve years in 1853. Then in the early 1860s Prussia negotiated a liberal commercial treaty with France and used this as leverage upon the other member states to accede to these terms. The *Zollverein* treaty was renewed from January 1866 on this liberal basis which was then also extended to Britain and other European countries [2: *Pt II*; 175; 188; 16: *501–4, 744 5, 888–9*].

None of this made political unification of any kind inevitable, let alone the particular form unification took. No one assumes today that the European Union will inevitably lead to a European state. It is possible for such economic associations to work simply because the constituent members each consider that they have more to gain through participation in such an association than through not participating. In that case the association works to coordinate and harmonise certain economic policies while individual states retain their sovereignty. Of course, the association does create greater interdependence and, especially when majority voting rather than unanimity is accepted, can undermine aspects of state sovereignty. However, there is one major respect in which analogies between the *Zollverein* and the European Union break down. In the case of the *Zollverein* one member state, namely Prussia, was far more powerful than all the other members put together. Furthermore, these states were also part of a political union – the *Bund* – which considerably restricted their sovereignty, although in the *Bund* they could, to a degree, balance Austria and Prussia against each other.

In another sense the analogy has more substance. Increased economic interdependence leads both to more intensified forms of cooperation and to conflict. Just as the European Union is in part animated by and in turn promotes ideas of Europeanism, so the *Zollverein* had similar effects on ideas of German unity which extended beyond commercial affairs. Already, for example, in 1847 a group of south German liberals drew up a programme which envisaged building German unity on the *Zollverein* [132, unit 3: *61*]. However, just as Europeanism takes different forms and also spawns anti-Europeanism, so too was this the case with such new ideas about German national organisation. To understand this better we need to turn to the field of cultural history.

[b] Culture

The main concern of this section is to try to establish how far and in what ways a national culture had been formed in Germany before unification and what might be the political implications of this.

Most people in early nineteenth-century Germany did not move very far from where they were born. Even in the growing cities the majority of immigrants came from within a 30-mile radius [16: *ch. 8*; 41; 96]. Germans were a relatively well-educated and literate population but most people did little reading. Bibles and almanacs are the most numerous of the books mentioned in wills and inventories [213; 184; 16: *ch. 8*; 219]. Most newspapers were largely concerned with local affairs or the activities of the particular state government. It was a major achievement when in 1847 some liberals succeeded in founding a newspaper with the word German in its title: the *Deutsche Zeitung*. The most important extensive institutions in which people regularly participated – the churches – expressed confessional values and identities which both transcended national boundaries (though this was more the case with Catholicism than Protestantism) and divided Germans. A Hamburg Lutheran had more in common with a Swedish Lutheran than with an Austrian Catholic. Individual states sought to cultivate loyalty towards themselves [173; 56; 33].

Not surprisingly, therefore, any sense that being German was important was weakly developed and confined to particular groups. Much attention has been paid to academics, teachers, pastors and civil servants, to their role in the cultivation of a national literature from the late eighteenth century and in formulating the argument that language and other aspects of a culture made nationality the basis of human identity [16: *ch. 9*; 55]. Leaving aside the debatable nature of that argument itself, it is generally agreed that this minority of intellectuals had little impact upon the vast majority of Germans [31].

This was the case even when the Napoleonic domination of Germany could be regarded as posing a common threat to Germans and, if only in anti-French terms, thereby stimulating a sense of German identity. The 'German War of Liberation' became an important element in later nationalist myth-making. In fact many Germans cooperated with the French, out of self-interest and because the French influence was seen to be progressive. Those who resisted the French (and most resistance came only after the failure of the Russian invasion had drastically weakened French control) did so for a mixture of motives in which a sense of German identity did not play an important role [31; 16: *chs 5 & 6*; 147; 47]. In terms of state resistance, for the *kleindeutsch* school there is the awkward fact that Austria fought against France more continuously and with more soldiers than did Prussia and in doing so also at times appealed to German national sentiments [115].

There were some nationalist organisations formed during and after the war of 1813–15. In parts of Germany, Catholic as well as Protestant, associations were formed to support the war effort. Gymnastic societies and volunteer corps gave practical expression to ideas of Germandom. Later war veterans' associations, student fraternities, choral societies, gymnastics and sharp-shooting clubs all sought to sustain the national ideal. For years afterwards the anniversary of the 'Battle of All Nations', that is, the battle of Leipzig of October 1813, was celebrated in many different German states [16: *ch.*

9; 179; 30]. A number of national memorials were constructed [202]. A wide range of festivals and anniversary celebrations could cultivate a sense of nationality, although these could have very different and often opposed political meanings [180; 190]. Yet only minorities of fairly well educated, young and mainly male Germans belonged to these associations and movements and took part in these festivals. They tended to be more important in Protestant than Catholic parts of Germany. Restored governments were suspicious of the threats such associations implied to their own authority and many were repressed after 1819.

However, the possibility of a national culture developing in new and important ways did exist. The general patterns of change in many parts of Germany helped create a more autonomous and extensive culture. Specialised educational institutions came to be much more important than before. Universities and other institutions of higher education increasingly trained people not merely for the traditional professions of law, medicine and the church but for new professions such as the civil service and engineering, and a range of new academic specialisms in the natural and social sciences [122]. Schooling expanded, especially in the growing towns [37; 140; 121].

This had an especial impact on people of middling positions in society. From the mid-century these broad social strata began to expand relative to the whole population. Given this trend, education could offer an important route up the social ladder for more and more people. The methods and content of education, especially in grammar schools (*Gymnasien*) and technical schools (*Realschule*) as well as universities, converged between different states, although Catholic areas did still often retain distinctive educational patterns. These people all read the same standard German (*Hochdeutsch*) language and had similar tastes in literature. The schools, in terms of curricula, teaching methods and public rhetoric (e.g. at anniversary ceremonies) increasingly expressed a pride in German nationality [196].

Apart from the influence of official institutions such as schools and universities there also developed a wide range of voluntary cultural associations in which this broad middle class predominated. Reading clubs encouraged common interests in literature; art societies developed to promote an interest in German art; music societies, especially men's choral societies, adopted similar repertoires of mainly German song and other music in different German states. (It is only

26

against this background that the success of that first pop star, Franz Liszt, can be understood.) These associations were not confined to the urban middle classes or to cultural activities. Associations with more practical purposes – for example, providing the benefits which later would become the responsibility of a welfare state – developed amongst urban workers and in many areas of the countryside. This may also have something to do with the decay of traditional organisations such as guilds and the patriarchal manor which were supposed to provide such benefits. Urban workers, especially skilled craftsmen, organised their own educational and sporting societies [44; 16; 130; 151; 30].

These associations had ulterior political purposes in periods when political organisation and discussion was forbidden. But they also served genuine cultural needs, as is demonstrated by their continued growth in the 1860s when there was much more political freedom. To them one can add more specialised professional associations such as those of German lawyers and German economists [157; 102]. Although many of these societies were local in membership and concern (e.g. the various history societies founded from the 1830s) they had a similar character; they often corresponded with one another; and increasingly they organised regional or national meetings and sometimes overarching associations. Local history societies, for example, cultivated contacts to the institution founded by Baron Stein, the *Monumenta Germania Historica*, set up to study medieval German history [210: *531–5*]. They also helped to develop a deeply historical view of German nationality [186; 38: *39–52*; 208: *chs 5 & 6*; 16: *542–55*].

The political potential of these associations first became clear during the 1848 revolution. Frequently it was the leaders of workers' educational associations and citizens' associations who became the party leaders of the period. Gymnastic societies became a major source of support for radicals. Rifle clubs contributed to the formation of citizen militias which were crucial to the battle for power in that year. In a world where mass political parties and media did not yet exist it was often an appeal to local traditions which could evoke support. It might limit the scope of political mobilisation but it also made political repression difficult. Yet this in turn pointed to the continued power of local identity; radicals found it diffiicult to make state-wide or national appeals [152 & 153; 216].

With political liberalisation from the late 1850s these cultural

27

movements expanded further. Their mutual connections and interests, as well as their concern with 'German' music, art and literature meant that they cultivated and embodied the idea of a German culture. This reached a climax in the celebration of the centenary of Schiller's birth in 1859. In towns all over Germany, and amongst German communities in many other parts of the world, there was a huge outpouring of sentiment for this German poet, and for the way in which Schiller was taken to embody a transcendent, quasi-religious conception of art, especially German art, over and beyond the mundane concerns of politics and everyday life [72; 204, 3; 207].

Many of these associations formed a popular basis for the liberal and radical national movement. That movement in turn encouraged these associations as providing a 'non-political' mass basis to their own, much smaller organisations [201; 158]. One of the most popular of the national liberals of the 1860s, Schulze-Delitzsch, made his name as an advocate and promoter of numerous associations, especially cooperatives and educational societies [167]. These embodied liberal and national ideals: they were voluntary, diffused across many states, and came together periodically at national congresses and festivals, celebrating German nationality and freedom [179; 16: ch. 13].

However, one cannot read any direct political significance into much of this. Such associations were divided between moderate and radical elements. Workers active in educational associations were angry when Schulze-Delitzsch advised them to remain aloof from politics and simply to regard themselves as 'honorary' members of the National Society (National Verein) which had been formed in 1859 to promote the cause of liberal nationalism and which charged a subscription beyond the pockets of workers [201; 176; 158: 432–80]. These associations were also divided between those who favoured a kleindeutsch and advocates of a grossdeutsch solution to the national question. Where these associations were most effective in mobilising a 'national' movement was when this was directed against external enemies, for example in the wave of enthusiasm for the cause of Schleswig-Holstein that was directed against Denmark and which swept many parts of Germany in 1863–4 [158: 206–28, 306–19].

The most popular associations – choral, gymnastic and sharp-shooting – appealed to more people than ever by the 1860s though this is to be measured in tens rather than hundreds of thousands. They were more important in Protestant than in Catholic areas. They were usually secular in character. There were movements which pointed in different directions, especially various Catholic social and cultural associations. Here one finds a similar concern with cultural and social issues, although perhaps social concerns loomed larger and the membership was more lower-class than that of the 'German' associations. These less well studied movements later helped underpin political Catholicism which looked with hostility upon the exclusion of Austria from Germany and which was to be very effective in mobilising anti-Prussian sentiment after 1866. The diffusion of these sentiments amongst a larger middling strata meant also that they lost much of the romantic and militant quality they had assumed immediately after 1815 and were now integrated into broader liberal currents of opinion. The opposition of the existing German states – non-national, monarchical and illiberal – to changes in the *status quo* also encouraged the view that liberal and national progress were two sides of the same coin [151; 163].

By the mid-1860s one could say that there was a large minority, mainly but not exclusively urban middle class and largely Protestant, which regarded itself as German and wanted to see greater national unity. This middle class had an increasing significance in the economy and also set the tone of public opinion as the producers and readers of an expanding newspaper and periodical literature. The key question is whether this opinion could be turned to political account.

[c] Power

Just as the dissolution of the European peace settlement with the Crimean war preceded the destruction of the *Bund* in 1866, so the putting together of that settlement in 1814–15 had created the essential conditions for the construction of the *Bund*. Metternich, the Austrian Chancellor and principal architect of the settlement of 1814–15, realised that it was impractical to undo much of what Napoleon had done with the German lands since 1803. To return to the Holy Roman Empire with its hundreds of statelets would be to return to a weak and discredited political order. In any case, it had been essential to bring most of Napoleon's German satellites over to the grand alliance which he organised in the summer of 1813 and to do that required a guarantee of their continued existence after the defeat of Napoleon. Only the King of Saxony failed to desert Napoleon

29

by the time the war resumed and he lost a large part of his kingdom in consequence [112 for this whole section].

This left little room for territorial manoeuvre at Vienna. It was easy enough to remove foreign princes, often members of Napoleon's family, and with them such creations as the Kingdom of Westphalia and the Duchy of Berg. Hannover was restored, partly on British insistence, partly as some kind of a balance to Prussia in northern Germany. Bavaria had to give up former Austrian territories and received in compensation the Palatinate, a Protestant enclave separated from the rest of Bavaria. Baden and Württemberg were largely confirmed in their possessions. Prussia received territory in central and western Germany as compensation for her Polish losses to Russia. The western gains considerably expanded former Hohenzollern possessions and made up the two provinces of Westphalia and the Rhinelands. In central Germany the northern part of Saxony was transferred to Prussia. There was a moment of tension when Prussia sought, with Russian support, to insist on the whole of Saxony but British and Austrian resistance prevented this. Austria did not seek fresh territorial gains in Germany. Indeed, she did not seek to regain Flanders which was incorporated into the Kingdom of the Netherlands and subsequently achieved independence as the constitutional monarchy of Belgium in 1830 (see Maps 1, 2 and 3).

There was the question of how these German states were to coordinate their policies. Restoration of the Holy Roman Empire or of the imperial title was impractical. Napoleon had provided a model in the Confederation of the Rhine of 1806. A new Confederation, the *Deutsche Bund*, was created. Externally the *Bund* was intended to provide a military deterrent to other powers, especially France. The fact that the Confederal Army achieved very little does not mean that this had not been seriously intended in 1815. The Confederation also forbade member states entering into military and diplomatic agreements with non-member states, though Austria and Prussia could evade this stipulation because they had territories outside the Confederation. The other German states had very little autonomy in the foreign policy and military fields.

One could regard the *Bund* primarily as a device for securing a shared control by Austria and Prussia of the other member states – some 37 of them ranging from medium states such as Bavaria, Hannover and Saxony to the city-republics of Bremen, Frankfurt, Hamburg and Lubeck. The *Bund* had a Diet which met in Frankfurt with votes related roughly to the size of the various states. Austria presided over the Diet. The rules of the *Bund* recommended that the different states draw up similar constitutions, allow people to move freely across state borders, and use the *Bund* to coordinate commercial affairs. None of this came to pass as each state asserted its own autonomy in these matters. However, in 1819 the enactment of the Carlsbad decrees ensured the imposition of common policing measures against liberal and national movements throughout the *Bund*, a process extended by further measures in the 1830s. In both cases Austria took the lead in initiating such repressive measures and Prussia willingly cooperated [16: *ch. 7*].

This earned the *Bund* the unenviable reputation of being nothing more than an oppressive policing system by which Austria and Prussia blocked the development of liberal and national movements throughout Germany. This is largely true despite recent efforts to write about the *Bund* more sympathetically [212; 217; 131]. However, the most important political developments took place in the individual states and the *Bund* could do little to influence those.

The medium states in particular represented a considerable change. They were larger and more independent than the myriad of small states they replaced. They had to work out ways of integrating new territories and subjects, especially those of different religious faiths. Protestant and Catholic rulers negotiated agreements with the Papacy. Protestant rulers recognised certain Catholic privileges; Catholic rulers did not allow the Papacy to exercise much control in their territories. In these ways the states of the *Bund* came to develop a much more secular, non-confessional identity than had been the case earlier.

Many of the states enacted constitutions, partly as a way of establishing a legitimate basis to their control of new possessions and also to give some kind of unitary structure to what were often very disparate territories. Baden, Bavaria and Württemberg considerably reformed the state administration and tried to establish a uniform state-wide authority. They also sought to eliminate political privileges, for example those of the *Standesherren*, formerly independent rulers of the Holy Roman Empire who were granted special privileges in 1814 [16: *chs 7 & 10*; for an English-language study of one state see 117].

Not all the medium states reformed with such zeal. Hannover sought to return to the aristocratic order of the old Electorate. The rump Kingdom of Saxony, despite or perhaps because of rapid economic growth, did not alter her political institutions. These and other states were compelled to move towards constitutional rule following the disturbances of 1830–1, though Hannover suspended that constitution in 1837. In other parts of northern and central Germany there was little constitutional or administrative reform until 1848.

There was less social and economic reform in the medium states, with the exception of Saxony. Guilds were restored; aristocratic privileges confirmed; towns often given the right to control who could become a citizen. Radicals in these states confined themselves purely to political demands, at the same time defending the rights of local communities to exclude outsiders from its privileges. Indeed, it was precisely this strong sense of community that provided the basis for radical challenges to state authority [159: *chs 9 & 10*; 16: *ch. 10*; 162].

Radical and confessional challenges in the individual states were more important problems than noisy student nationalism. *Bund* policing could help the small and medium states. However, it also had the effect of 'nationalising' political opposition. Opponents of state governments constantly found that behind those governments stood the *Bund*. That made national reform a necessary condition of state reform. Gradually political opponents of individual states took up connections with one another. By 1847 such opponents, largely concentrated in southern and south-western Germany, had coalesced into two loose camps. Radicals looked to an appeal to the 'German people' as the way forward. Liberals, concerned to establish freer institutions but suspicious of popular politics, turned to the *Zollverein* as a vehicle for reform, though this appeared a rather contrived idea. More generally they hoped to be able to cooperate with reforming rulers [150: *ch. 3*; 146: *ch. 3*; 197: *20–38*].

The collapse of the governments of the small and medium states in early 1848 demonstrated just how much they had depended upon Austro-Prussian support. Radical attempts to seize control were defeated and new liberal ministries were formed. Much political energy in 1848–9 was confined to seeking change within individual states. However, the concern with national reform was also taken in hand. On the basis of popular elections throughout Germany deputies to a German National Assembly met in Frankfurt in May 1848. Their task was to draw up a constitution for a German nation-state [for background see 216 & 154].

The Frankfurt parliament faced formidable problems. It had no civil service or army and it was unclear on what, let alone how, it should base its authority. It did eventually create a German Provisional Authority but it always recognised that it had to work through, not against, the individual states, especially Austria and Prussia.

It was a completely new assembly without any established procedures. It took time for deputies to sort out their political goals and begin organising in a loose party-like manner. The majority of the deputies were of a liberal persuasion although this covered a wide range of positions. It seemed sensible to wait to see how the politics of the individual states evolved, especially in Austria and Prussia, before moving on to politically contentious issues which might offend those states. One could not assume that an Austria or a Prussia with liberal ministries and their own constituent assemblies would be any more amenable to external interference than the old dynasties.

Consequently the German National Assembly began its constitutional work by drawing up a section concerned with the rights of German citizens rather than addressing the 'practical' questions of national institutions and territory. The debates and decisions on this matter are fascinating both for what they reveal of how much had to be done before the idea of being a 'German' acquired any real substance and as an insight into the liberal sentiments and concerns of the time [29: *ch. 6*].

Only in the autumn of 1848 did the Assembly turn to the central political questions. The tragedy was that by this time the counter-revolution was advancing rapidly in both Austria and Prussia and the German National Assembly was squeezed between these counter-revolutions. It was impossible to resolve the issue of Austria or Prussia. Austrian deputies took the *grossdeutsch* position and Prussian deputies the *kleindeutsch* one, although Prussian deputies who were Catholic were more likely to favour the *grossdeutsch* position. Deputies from other parts of Germany tended to divide on the basis of how radical they were or their religion. Forced to choose, a majority made up of *kleindeutsch* and radical deputies offered the hereditary emperorship of Germany to the King of Prussia [29: *ch. 8*; 216: *ch. 9*].

Frederick William IV rejected the offer, partly because of a constitution which was in any case too radical, partly because of the need to gain support from other princes, but mainly through fear of war with Austria. That spelt the end of the German National Assembly. Radicals sought to mobilise support for the imperial

33

constitution in some of the smaller states but these were repressed by June 1849. Prussia did, however, seek to obtain support from more moderate liberals for the creation of a Prussian-dominated association of states in northern and central Germany. Austria was still preoccupied with restoring order elsewhere in the empire and the medium states were pressed into negotiating with Prussia in 1849–50 to establish a political authority under Prussian leadership. However, they soon took the opportunity to distance themselves from this as Austria reasserted herself in Germany. That reassertion partly took the form of presenting a different plan of reform, the idea of the whole of the Habsburg Empire entering both the *Bund* and the *Zollverein*. Some of the medium states were politically attracted to the broader Customs Union but this was economically impractical. There was less enthusiasm for expanding the *Bund* as that could lead to Austrian domination. In any case, Prussia was as opposed to this as Austria had been to Prussian plans for a narrower political union in the north. Both plans were dropped by early 1851, although not before Austria had compelled Prussia, by threat of war, to give up her plans for leadership in Germany. (The Prussian climbdown on 29/30 November 1850 is sometimes referred to as the humiliation of Olmütz, that being the place where the final agreement was reached.) [177; 178: *24–38, 85–91*.]

The issue of political reform in Germany died for a decade. Individual German states went about restoring the old order in the 1850s. Especially where soldiers had violently put down radical movements there was genuine repression. Elsewhere the atmosphere was somewhat freer [216: *204–28*]. Yet some states felt it necessary to make concessions to some of the demands of 1848–9. In Prussia and Austria, for example, authoritarian states also permitted far greater economic freedom. The economic growth of the time probably also defused resentment and made it easier to maintain stability [89]. Only towards the end of the decade did ideas of national reform once again become a matter of public discussion. One can look at this at two different 'German' levels: the development of a broad national movement and the policies of the medium states [146: *ch. 3*; 97; 116].

Those wishing to promote national unity had learnt some fundamental lessons from the failure of 1848–9. One needed power, not merely fine sentiments, in order to fashion greater national unity. The 'German people' were largely indifferent to the cause of national unity, especially if that meant the imposition of new institutions upon them, and even those who favoured such unity were divided about the form it should take. The Austrian government, in order to maintain the integrity of its multinational empire and ensure its pre-eminence in Germany, was an inveterate enemy of any serious plan to form a national state. After 1848 to take up a *grossdeutsch* position more often meant opposing the *kleindeutsch* position than a genuine and practical commitment to real national reform.

The result of this learning process can be seen in the National Society (*National Verein*) which was founded in 1859. This followed the onset of the New Era in Prussia, the very recent example of the success of the Italian national movement and the consequent erosion of Austrian power. The *National Verein* had branches in many different German states, although more in the north than the south. It looked to Prussia to lead the way towards national unity. However, it hoped and assumed that this would be achieved peacefully; Prussia had to make 'moral conquests' in Germany. This language was very much in the fashion in the New Era and had even been used by the Prince Regent (later King) William. It was assumed that only a liberal Prussian state could pursue the right kind of policies and create this climate of opinion in the rest of Germany. In the New Era from 1858 (see below, chapter 4) Prussia did seem to be pursuing such a policy. Equally important, changes in other German states seemed to support this liberal and national movement. Many significant liberal reforms were introduced in the late 1850s and early 1860s in such areas as guild reform and commercial agreements. Liberals entered governments, most notably in Baden which represented a south German outpost of pro-Prussian national liberalism. The *National Verein* brought together progressive middle-class opinion on a national level and played a powerful part in shaping educated public opinion [201; 36; 158].

Furthermore, the *National Verein* had close links with liberal parties in the individual states. It could appeal to a kind of mass support in its links to various cultural and social associations described in the previous section. It strongly influenced the political values expressed by some of the major newspapers and periodicals of the time. At the same time the economic growth of the period induced liberals to believe that political unity was but the next step in the progressive movement of history. The middle class was leading the way in both the conquest of nature and the destruction of reactionary elements in society and achieving national unity was an integral part of this process.

There were tensions within the *National Verein* and the broader national movement. The more radical wing of the movement still cherished ideas of building up a head of popular pressure as a means of compelling governments to pursue more national policies. These elements had sufficient influence to get the *National Verein* to proclaim the enactment of the democratic Imperial Constitution of 1849 as its goal. However, more moderate elements were always sceptical about this commitment and managed to prevent the *National Verein* becoming a mass organisation. Its membership by 1862 peaked at about 25,000.

The whole national movement was flung into disarray by the constitutional crisis in Prussia which derailed its basic political strategy. It was shocked by the appointment of Bismarck as Minister-President in September 1862 because this seemed to block the path towards unity mapped out by the *National Verein*.

The national movement was not confined to the *National Verein*. There were German nationalists who still wished to see Austria pre-eminent in Germany or at least still associated with a future German state. These came together in December 1862 to form the *Reform Verein* [97: *ch. 1*]. This organisation became particularly active when it was a question of supporting Austrian policies of federal reform designed to appeal to the national movement. The bulk of its membership came from parts of central Germany which felt most threatened by Prussia. It was much more dependent upon the Austrian government than the *National Verein* was upon the Prussian government, partly because it had no conception of how desirable political change could come about except through Austrian action but also because it did not develop a critical view of what should happen in Austria in order to produce the appropriate policies. Internal political differences were larger than in the *National Verein*. There were conservatives who thought primarily in terms of the preservation of the *Bund* and radicals who envisaged a more unified and democratic Germany which included Austrian Germany [97].

Most of the medium states had welcomed the restoration of the *Bund* in 1851. This removed the threat of Prussian dominance which had been posed in 1849–50. These governments already found themselves falling under Prussian domination within the *Zollverein*. When they sought to challenge this dominance, either on commercial grounds (usually protectionism in the south German states) or on political grounds (wishing to see Austria as a member in order to balance Prussian influence) they found that Prussia was too powerful economically and they were too dependent upon the *Zollverein* to be able to resist Prussian policy. Indeed, their own publics often impressed that dependency upon them [188; 75].

This meant that generally the medium states, especially in central and southern Germany, supported Austria within the Confederation and usually allied with her to ward off Prussian threats. This happened, for example, in 1861–3. In December 1861 Prussia circulated a note to the various German courts which revived fears of the 'narrower union' she had pursued in 1849–50. Immediately the response of many of the other states was to look to Austria for a rejection of this policy. This was soon made clear in a rejoinder of 2 February 1862 which was signed not just by Austria but also by the kingdoms of Bavaria, Hannover, Saxony and Württemberg and the two Hessian states [4: 31]. (Generally on the *Bund* in the 1860s and issues of reform see [143 & 111].)

Yet that did not mean that these states would always be pro-Austrian. When Austria followed up on this rejection of Prussian policy with an outline of her own ideas for federal reform these ideas soon ran into resistance at the Federal Diet, not merely from Prussia but also from other states. When Austria changed tack and called together a princes' congress in August 1863 – one which King William refused to attend on Bismarck's insistence – there was little liking for a scheme which would increase Austrian influence over other states. The medium states did not have to oppose this openly; they could depend upon Prussia doing that for them.

The other states also sometimes initiated their own ideas of federal reform [97]. They were at one with the national movement in supporting the Augustenberg cause in Schleswig-Holstein as that would have created another medium state and increased their influence within the *Bund*. With the important exception of Baden, the medium states opposed an increase in either Prussian or Austrian influence in the rest of Germany. At the same time, their own individual conflicts and different concerns, as well as their lack of power, meant that they never managed to put forward any concerted policy of reform.

The national movement was riven by differences between moderates and liberals, *kleindeutsch* and *grossdeutsch*. However, there was generally a far greater weight of opinion in favour of some kind of Prussian leadership. This had lost ground to some extent with the constitutional crisis. By the end of 1862 the national movement was not sure of how it was to make any progress on the national question. Its moderates opposed outright resistance to Bismarck's rule (e.g. the idea of a tax boycott) while its radicals made it impossible to collaborate with existing conservative regimes. The medium states tacked between Austria and Prussia. It was, therefore, the policies of these two states which would be of crucial importance.

[iii] Austria

The hindsight historians enjoy is a mixed blessing. We know what happened next but this can also distort our vision. The story of German unification is usually written as the rise of Prussia and the decline of Austria. There is a strong temptation to see this decline as inevitable and to discern symptoms of it in every aspect of Austrian history. I will try to avoid doing this.

[a] Economics

The generally held assumption for a long time was that Austria had a backward and slow-growth economy. Much recent research, however, has shown this to be misleading. [Generally for this whole section see 98; 84; 135: *222–9*; 16: *744–7*; 14: *ch. 2.*] About 70 per cent of the population was dependent upon agriculture. In many parts of the empire land was cultivated on a collective basis, food was produced for local consumption, and noble landowners possessed many privileges and wielded great power. This changed markedly in 1848 when the revolution helped to bring about peasant emancipation, although largely along lines which favoured noble landowners [50: *ch. 17*; 49: *41–4, 203–38*; 125: *273–96*].

There was rapid economic development in some regions. In some areas in the eastern (Transleithian) half of the empire commercial agriculture developed, stimulated by the demand for food from western Europe. In Lombardy, under Austrian control until 1859, rich lands and commercial agriculture created a lucrative tax base for the imperial government. There were regions of industrial growth, especially in northern parts of Bohemia and Moravia with coal mining, metal

38

and textile production being of particular importance. Vienna grew rapidly and attracted a good deal of industry. The removal of internal tariffs was intended to increase intra-regional trade and encourage specialisation [125: *296–316*].

Austria was distanced from the most rapidly growing trade routes which led north and west across Europe to the Baltic and North Sea and on to the Atlantic. But some regions had access to good river routes, especially if internal road and canal improvements were pushed forward. There was considerable railway building in some regions and schemes (or dreams) of finding alternative routes to the New World, for example with railways to Italian ports such as Genoa and thence into the Mediterranean. In this regard the loss of Lombardy and influence in Italy was a major economic blow.

The economy of Austria, especially the western half, only came to fall behind that of the rest of Germany from around 1860, but this was due to the exceptionally high growth rate in Prussia–Germany in the following decade. Austrian economic performance compared favourably with that of France and was more impressive than what was happening in Russia. Few historians have suggested that the disparity with Prussia automatically rendered Russia or France politically and militarily weaker than Prussia. Why and how relative economic backwardness might produce such effects requires separate consideration.

In one important respect the disparity weakened Austria's position in Germany and this was in relation to the *Zollverein*. We have seen that Austria unsuccessfully tried to get into the *Zollverein* in the early 1850s and again in the mid-1860s. She had the support of the majority of the members of the *Zollverein*. The stumbling block was her economic weakness which would not allow her to accept the low tariff policy dictated by Prussia. Austria did nevertheless secure agreements with the *Zollverein* which reduced mutual tariff barriers, gave her some preferential tariffs over other outside states and provided her with most-favoured-nation status. (This meant that if and when the *Zollverein* concluded agreements with third states which lowered tariffs on particular imports into the *Zollverein*, those new tariffs were automatically extended to Austrian products.) As a consequence the proportion of Austrian import and export trade with the *Zollverein* grew steadily in the 1850s and 1860s [16: *745–6*].

Zollverein politics points to one way in which economic power can be expressed politically. There are three other aspects to be considered: the fiscal, military and domestic political consequences.

In principle a more rapidly growing economy could provide greater government revenue which can boost state power, above all by supporting a large and well-equipped army. The problem Austria faced here was that her administration, in a highly regionalised economy and political system, was much less efficient than that of Prussia in tapping these resources. Austrian state finance was in crisis from the time of the Crimean war and in the 1860s military expenditure was going down, not up.

More direct military consequences of economic growth were to do with the provision of railways, modern communications and a capacity to produce new weapons. Economic historians are right to point to the relatively good growth rates of the Austrian economy in the mid-nineteenth century but compared to Prussia after 1855 this was much more in the field of consumer than capital goods (see Table I and compare the key outputs of coal and steel). Relative to Prussia the Austrian railway network fell behind in the 1860s.

Finally, one should note the very patchy nature of Austrian growth. There were huge disparities between the most backward and the most advanced regions. The growth and *per capita* income figures sink dramatically once one includes the Hungarian half of the empire. The new interests associated with this economic growth lacked influence; Magyar magnates counted for more in imperial politics than did Bohemian mineowners.

In all these respects one can conclude that from around 1860, despite a generally favourable trend of economic development, the economic underpinnings of state power were shifting against Austria and in favour of Prussia.

[b] Culture

Germany had (and has) no dominant cultural centre like London or Paris. Different states promoted their own university towns and capital cities. However, in 1815 most Germans would have chosen Vienna, venue for a peace conference which was also a glittering social occasion, as the leading German city. By contrast, Berlin had been deserted by its monarch and court in 1806–7 and only established a university in 1810. By mid-century Berlin had reached comparable size to Vienna and was beginning to engage in prestige building programmes. Yet in the 1850s Austria, quite consciously as part of her claim to leadership within Germany, began a major rebuilding drive in Vienna comparable to that carried through in Paris at the same time [199: *357–70*].

Vienna, however, was an imperial, not a national capital. The Germans of the Habsburg Empire, especially the nobility and upper bourgeoisie who staffed its army and administration, saw themselves as the dominant cultural group within a multinational empire whose mission was both to maintain Austrian pre-eminence within Germany and to ensure German predominance in south-eastern Europe. A strong sense of national consciousness – which increased in intensity in conflict with that of other nationalities – did not lead Austrian Germans towards the idea of a German nation-state but rather towards ideas of new forms of imperial control. In many regions until mid-century at least national consciousness did not carry political connotations. A Bohemian might speak Czech or German at home and German in public and these could be seen as complementary, not opposed [104, I: *ch. 3*; 70: *chs 1 & 2*].

Furthermore, Austrian Germany was a Catholic culture. Protestants might acquire high position but they were a very small minority. In the 1850s and early 1860s, a more secular and bourgeois German elite did achieve greater influence and this can help account for the more assertive and effective role Austria played in Germany in this period. However, from the decline of Schmerling's influence in 1863 there was a tendency to return to more decentralised forms of control in which Catholic aristocrats and the church played a more important role. A good deal of cultural, educational and charitable activity which in Protestant Germany was organised through secular and voluntary associations, in Austria was instead channelled through the manifold institutions of the Catholic church. This reduced the likelihood of such associations forming the cultural basis of support for a more outward looking national movement. One should not exaggerate this. There were, for example in Vienna, choral, gymnastic and educational associations which took up connections with their counterparts in other German states and attended annual festivals. The Schiller centenary was celebrated in Vienna. However, there was nothing like the same density of such 'German' cultural activity. Finally, Germans in many parts of the Habsburg Empire were placed on the defensive by the assertions of cultural if not political claims from hitherto culturally subordinate groups such as the Czechs. In 1848 these claims were to crystallise

41

into political forms, albeit only the concern of a small minority [104, I: *ch. 5* for the Czechs].

Austria continued to absorb elements from German culture elsewhere but perhaps had a decreasing influence beyond its boundaries. For example, it is interesting to observe that there was still a pattern, up to and beyond 1866, of Germans from other states coming into Austrian service. The Counsellor for German Affairs from 1852 to 1872, Biegeleben, who was one of the most important foreign-policymakers in Vienna, had been born in Darmstadt and served in the government established by Archduke John in Frankfurt in 1848 before coming into Austrian service. After the defeat of 1866 Austria turned to the Prime Minister of Saxony, Count Beust, to lead her affairs. But Austrians did not tend to go and serve other governments. By contrast in Prussia, Germans born outside Prussia, especially Catholics, seemed to be of decreasing importance in political affairs. Bernstorff, a Danish German and Foreign Minister in the early 1830s, was one of the last such people to serve as a minister though Moltke does fall into this category. Bismarck in his reminiscences insinuates that the Catholic Radowitz led Prussia astray in the period 1849–51 because of his Catholicism and a stress upon a German mission rather than the need to retain a strong, traditional order in Prussia [226: *50, 64–5*; 227, I: *49–50, 70–2*]. In this sense, although ties of dynasty and nobility maintained family links across the German states, including between Austria and Prussia, there was perhaps a growing apart, partly based on confession and partly on state membership. Austria remained more 'German' in the sense of importing elite members from the medium states; Prussia was developing a sharper state- and territory-centred elite [105: *49–50*].

The *Zollverein* intensified economic transactions between the member states far more than between those states and Austria, even if Austrian trade with the rest of Germany did grow steadily. We know a little about patterns of communications in terms of newspaper circulation and the sending of letters and the making of journeys, and these displayed similar trends [105: *63, 79*; 16: *744*].

Austrian Germans did not wish to choose between their national and their imperial identities but to combine them. Would their fellow Germans and the other nationalities of the empire let them do this?

[c] Power

This dilemma expressed itself most clearly in politics. In 1814–15 Metternich had devised a conservative system of Austrian pre-eminence. This depended upon the operation of dualism with Prussia in Germany and the maintenance of conservative alliances with the other great powers in Europe. In this way Austria managed to remain the leading German power and to keep her diverse and sprawling empire. Three things could undermine this achievement: the position in Germany; the relationships with the other major powers; the internal situation of the empire.

We have seen that in Germany by 1860 the economic balance of power was shifting away from Austria, the greater part of the national movement looked to Prussia for leadership, and Austrian Germans tended to be marginalised within a Protestant-flavoured national cultural movement. From the time of the Crimean war Austria began to find herself diplomatically isolated, especially from Russia. In 1859 she fought France and Piedmont alone; there was no conservative alliance upon which she could call to maintain the *status quo*. More generally Austria suffered from what has been termed 'imperial overstretch', that is, she had a very broad range of commitments which were increasingly difficult to prioritise, coordinate and maintain. (Kennedy [15] coined the term; Carr [20: *62*] applies it to Austria.) In so far as she had economic difficulties these might be seen more as the result of her geopolitical and military commitments rather than as the principal cause of decline [98: *51–3*].

Furthermore Austria's government faced difficulties in maintaining control over her diverse territories. For a moment in the summer of 1848 it seemed that the Habsburg Empire might fall apart. Hungary had virtually declared independence; Austrian troops had been forced out of most of northern Italy; the court had abandoned Vienna to radicals. The Habsburg recovery was due not only to the efforts of her army and loyal German subjects but also to the exploitation of nationality conflicts (Romanians and Croatians against Magyars, Germans against Czechs) and to assistance from the Russians. It also helped that the various opponents of the Habsburgs failed to cooperate with one another [118: *322–425*; 104, II: *3–39*; 149; 76; 138; 133; 114].

After 1848 repression led to centralised bureaucratic rule from Vienna. All the subject nationalities, including those who had supported

43

the Habsburgs in 1848–9, were dismayed by this policy [104, II: 25–87; 118: 426–94]. As soon as international crises arose, the fragility of this system of rule revealed itself. Following the defeat in the war of 1859 the government had begun a process of administrative devolution, one effect of which was to considerably increase Magyar power in the eastern half of the empire. Lombardy, the Habsburg's richest province, was lost. The costs of war had multiplied public debt to enormous proportions. That in turn made the government reluctant to embark on further military modernisation just as Prussia began to do so [148]. The Austrian military budget virtually halved between 1860 and 1865 (Table I). The financial crisis also made the regime more susceptible to pressure for constitutional reform if the conservative policy of devolution faltered.

The return to constitutional government and greater centralisation, at the very least in the western half of the empire, came with the appointment of Schmerling as chief minister in December 1860. Schmerling had a *großdeutsch* reputation extending back to his period as a deputy in the Frankfurt parliament in 1848–9. He was one of those self-confident high bourgeois Austrian Germans who believed that enlightened government under constitutional rules could bind the empire more closely together and could be linked to a strong forward policy in Germany [104, II: *115–25*]. In February 1861 he introduced a new constitution for the empire designed to provide the basis for this policy. Whether the Magyars in particular, especially after the shift back to administrative devolution had put them in firm control of local government in their region, could be persuaded to participate in such a project was doubtful. In any case the policy was not consistently backed by the Emperor Franz Joseph and probably had little chance of success given the international and financial crises into which the government was plunged [118: *495–568*; 104, II: *ch. 19*; 48: *116–23*]. The success of constitutionalism depended on building good relations between the government and the elites in new representative institutions. Financial burdens caused by military expansion and war would undermine the development of such relations [14: *333–43*].

All of this conditioned Austria's policy in Germany. Austria had two options. One was to try to maintain the *status quo* through the policy of Austro-Prussian dualism. The problem was whether Austria could compel Prussia to stay with that policy. The other option was to pursue a forward policy in Germany, promoting federal reform with a view to making Austria the dominant element. One could call these the Metternich and the Schwarzenberg options after their two most noted proponents in the periods 1815–48 and 1848–53 respectively. The first tended to be associated with the maintenance of alliances with conservative powers and a lack of domestic political reform while the second was linked to a more unilateral diplomacy and a domestic reform programme designed to boost economic growth and strengthen central government [40].

After Schwarzenberg's death Austria never pursued one or other of these policies consistently. Partly that was because tactically they were closely related. For example, threatening Prussia with an assertive German policy could serve as a means of forcing Prussia to move back to dualism. Partly it was because different interests in the Austrian government favoured one or the other policy. Schmerling, for example, wanted to pursue an aggressive policy and thought it would also help his constitutional project. The Foreign Minister until October 1864, Rechberg, was more inclined to try to work with Prussia. Partly it was because the alternatives were not clearly formulated. The Schwarzenberg option had emerged more as part of an aggressive counter-revolution both within the empire and Germany. But counter-revolution tends to end when the revolution has been defeated. Thus there was a tendency to slip back into Metternichian mode, although the conditions for such a policy were less favourable from the mid-1850s than they had been before 1848 [4: *39*; 79; 5 & 40].

One thing was clear in 1860: Austria would not give up her position in Germany without a fight. The loss of Lombardy, if anything, had hardened that resolution. The removal or even substantial reduction of Austrian influence in Germany would spell the end of her position as a great power. In 1862–3 Austria actually asserted herself in Germany, taking advantage of the constitutional crisis in Prussia. In 1862 she floated the idea of federal reform in the Federal Diet. When that did not prosper, the government hit upon the idea of a great meeting of all the German princes to discuss federal reform. The congress met in August 1863, only the King of Prussia remaining absent. At this point it did appear that the tendency to look to Berlin rather than Vienna for liberal and national leadership was misplaced.

However, apart from the hostility of Prussia and the doubts of the medium German states, there were also internal opponents of this policy. Magyars, above all, had no interest in Germany and could expect to play a more important role, both in their own part of the empire and in the central government, if Austria was forced out of Germany. There were Austrian Germans who doubted the wisdom of abandoning the dualist approach. In addition, the new kingdom of Italy aimed to acquire the Austrian province of Venetia. In turn her patron, France, contemplated how she could gain from a crisis in Germany. That could only happen if the other German power also asserted herself in Germany.

[iv] Prussia

[a] Economics

Up to the 1840s Prussia experienced little modern industrial growth. Her agriculture had been more thoroughly reformed than in any other part of Germany and this had contributed to rapid increases in productivity and production which in turn sustained considerable demographic growth. Manufacturing in such sectors as textiles, metals and building also increased, and there were impressive advances in regional specialisation and commercial production for distant markets. However, there was little technological innovation, most output was for the final consumer, and craft workshop or domestic production far outweighed factories and mines. The agricultural labour force only began to decline relative to the total labour force after mid-century [see Table I; 11: *ch. 6*; 52].

The *Zollverein* originated with Prussia's commitment to integrating the economies of her two western provinces with the rest of the state. Many sectors of the Prussian economy, including food-exporting regions in the east, stood to gain from commercial liberalisation. There were powerful elements in government who believed that a free market economy was the best recipe for development as well as a way of reducing government expenditure. Accordingly the government reduced its own intervention in the economy and society and also attacked economic privileges such as those associated with guilds, noble landholding and fiscal-legal distinctions between town and countryside. A large customs union fitted well into this policy as it would further encourage regional specialisation and increase taxable trade flows. It was also fiscally attractive, even after Prussia had made generous concessions to other states, because it simplified and reduced customs administration. These, rather than political considerations, weighed most with Prussian policymakers to mid-century [188: *43–87*; 127].

There were signs of change in the 1840s, above all with a sharp rise in investment levels, much of which was directed to railway building, and the stimulus this gave to coal and iron production. Railway building involved large-scale capital investment, close business–government links (if only to obtain permission and to acquire the land needed), and the employment of large numbers of workers, even if this was only a transitory labour force. Coal production shifted to deep-shaft mining which required greater concentrations of capital and labour. Iron-smelting shifted from a charcoal- to a coke-fired base with similar effects. After 1848 the government encouraged further growth in these directions by removing its restrictions upon the formation of limited liability companies and the operations of private mineowners. From the mid-1850s the economy began to grow rapidly, only mildly affected by a commercial crisis in 1857–8, entering into a boom in the 1860s which only came to an end in 1873–4. Industrialisation now was led by large-scale investment in capital goods production, centralised production and technological innovation, although there were also great increases in certain types of consumer goods production such as textiles. Such an economy could directly strengthen the Prussian state by providing it with leverage over satellite economies, the capability of moving soldiers and military supplies much more quickly than before and technical capacities to design and mass produce new weapons. This was a marked change from a time when the main political effects of a successful economy were fiscal, that is how much money could be extracted from it for state purposes.

There clearly were fiscal benefits as well. The extra military expenditure coincided with a period of economic growth and did not, therefore, spark off the same discontent as it might have done if this had been a period of stagnation or recession. The liberals opposed the military budget for political, not economic, reasons and could not mobilise popular support behind their opposition. The economic elites that expanded with economic growth approved of much government policy and had a strong interest in seeing Prussia integrate the rest of Germany more effectively. Their disagreements with the government were more to do with its lack of accountability and scepticism about the capacity of conservative officials to pursue the correct domestic and German policies. If Bismarck could provide reassurances on those matters, business interests would support the regime.

By 1860 Prussian economic pre-eminence in Germany was clear. It dominated the *Zollverein* which tied virtually all of non-Austrian Germany to its leadership [110]. The 1860s was the decade which saw the fastest economic growth in Prussia during the nineteenth century. The question was whether this economic dynamism and leadership could be converted into cultural, political and military forms.

[b] Culture

By 1850 Berlin was no longer a garrison capital dominated by soldiers and bureaucrats. The university had become one of the most prestigious in the world, especially admired for the way in which it promoted research and new disciplines at the expense of training in the traditional professions. There was great respect for Prussian achievements in the field of technical education and her system of elementary and secondary education. Many foreigners regarded the Prussian administration as the most efficient and least corrupt in Europe. The scaling down of the Prussian army since 1830 reduced her militarist reputation. The stereotype of the German in mid-century was that of a dreamy poet or unworldly philosopher, not of an arrogant soldier or a dynamic entrepreneur.

There was also much to criticise. The economic transformation had profound social consequences – many noble manors were now owned by non-nobles and there had developed both a professional and an economic upper middle class of great wealth and prestige. Furthermore, an increasingly independent and commercially minded peasantry was not prepared to accept the partial and incompetent rule of a declining nobility. The big cities and the more advanced provinces like the Rhinelands generated a larger middle class and a popular demand for a more equal and participatory society. Nevertheless, especially after the repression of the 1848 revolution, power remained in the hands of a declining aristocratic elite which seemed out of touch, even hostile, to the changes that were placing Prussia in a powerful position in Germany. The new mood of optimism and progress might have gained control in much of the economy and in many new cultural institutions, but if anything that created even more resentment that the state itself was so resistant to change.

Expression was given to this resentment through a powerful liberal movement. The spokesmen of this movement prided themselves on their realism, unlike the dreamers of 1848. It was one of their number, Rochau, who coined the term *Realpolitik* not as a mark of cynicism but rather to insist that power must ally itself with the forces of progress or be swept aside. A great deal of the secular/ Protestant cultural organisation that I have already described (see above, pp. 26–9) was centred upon Prussia. Anderson cites a newspaper article of March 1861 written by a resident of the small East Prussian town of Gumbinnen who doubted whether a Schiller Association could be established there because of the large number of associations (*Vereine*) already in existence.

Artisan Verein, Choral Verein, National Verein, Charity Verein, Orphan Verein, Credit Verein, Peace Verein, Gustavus Adolphus Verein [an evangelical Protestant association], Agricultural Verein, Bible Society, Town Club, lodges, and other Vereins already existed. The article spoke of 'a certain Verein satiation'. [36: *304*]

The same story can be told of numerous towns and cities throughout Prussia. The organising drive extended to more purely economic organisations – chambers of commerce, commercial associations and special business interest groups – which numbered in the hundreds in Prussia in the early 1860s. About half the membership of the *National Verein* was located in Prussia. No wonder liberal spokesmen considered that their victory was but a matter of time; it was inscribed in the economic and cultural progress of the day and remained only to be translated into political form.

[c] Power

The settlement of 1814–15 turned Prussia towards Germany. She lost many of her Polish possessions and received in compensation land in central and western Germany. There was no question of reviving that eastern mission. Prussian advances, if there were to be any, had to be in Germany. Whereas Austria had many commitments outside Germany, Prussia could only look to Germany.

That did not mean that she *would* do so. For a long time Prussia seemed content to accept the arrangements of 1814–15, including Austrian pre-eminence in Germany. She had enough problems coming to terms with the effects of the Napoleonic wars. The army was reduced along with public debt, and many reforms, especially in the field of agriculture, were carried through. An ambitious foreign policy would have cost money and that would have required constitutional concessions in order to raise revenue. That was a hard choice for the monarchy to make as became clear when a United Diet was summoned in 1847. The reason for this was that the government wished to borrow money for a railway-building project and constitutional agreements made in the 1820s required that the provincial diets be brought together in a single assembly. When the Diet demanded a state-wide constitution as its price for agreeing a loan, Frederick William IV dissolved it, declaring that he did not wish a piece of paper to come between him and his people.

1848 was both a threat and an opportunity. At the same moment that Frederick William IV agreed to grant freedoms such as those of the press and assembly and to set in motion a process leading to constitutional government, he also declared that Prussia would 'go forth into Germany'. This could be seen as an attempt to channel Prussian energies outwards and to take advantage of the collapse of other German governments including Austria.

In fact, most energy was devoted to internal problems during 1848, following the collapse of crown authority in late March. By November the king had regained the initiative and removed the Prussian National Assembly from Berlin. In December he issued his own constitution. In April 1849 he rejected the offer of the imperial crown made to him by the German National Assembly. At the same time he tried, both with governments and moderate nationalists, to extend Prussian control over other parts of northern and central Germany. However, Austrian recovery and the pursuit of an aggressive policy by Schwarzenberg, along with the clear desire of other German governments not to fall under Prussian influence, compelled Prussia to give up this policy at Olmütz in November 1850 [16: 710–15; 177].

From 1850 government was in the hands of an aristocratic elite of high officials and army officers. The relatively democratic constitution of 1848 was unilaterally amended in an authoritarian direction in 1850. The Upper House (*Herrenhaus*) was dominated by the old nobility. The Lower House (*Landtag*) was to be elected on the basis of a three-class voting system which divided the electorate (all adult males) of each constituency into three groups with equal tax liabilities. Each of these three classes, voting in public, elected the same number of electors. These electors then chose the representative for the constituency. It can be argued that this franchise favoured wealth rather than privilege, and in that sense was not a traditional conservative measure. Nevertheless, the result was profoundly anti-democratic and that helps to explain the poor turnouts in the lower electoral classes. Furthermore, manipulation of these elections produced a pliable lower house until the end of the 1850s [36: *ch. 8*].

The officials in power in Berlin, all highly conservative, were generally reluctant to challenge the *status quo* in Germany. They were well aware of their lack of popular or middle-class support in Prussia and associated policies of national reform with the demands of their political opponents. After Olmütz their main concern was no more than that Austria respect Prussia's rights and status. For example, during the Crimean war, the Prussian government did not meekly support Austrian policy but neither did she seek to exploit Austrian difficulties as Bismarck advised. Reaction at home; dualism in Germany: this was to be the order of the day.

This policy did not change much with the New Era. In 1858 Wilhelm became Prince-Regent when the king's mental instability had clearly rendered him unfit to continue to rule. He succeeded as king when Frederick William died in January 1861. William had never expected to be king. He was above all a military man. At the same time he had little sympathy for the conservative clique which had run affairs in the 1850s. He insisted on an end to electoral manipulation and in 1858 election results produced a moderate liberal majority in the *Landtag*. William was happy to bring such moderates into his government. Liberals were now hopeful that this would lead to further liberal measures at home and a more assertive policy in Germany. The effect of constitutional government since December 1848, despite its limitations, had been to create state-wide political organisation and connections focused on parliament with which a reform-minded ruler could come to some understanding.

Liberals were soon disappointed. In 1859 the Prussian government was divided on how to respond to the Italian war. On the one hand there were those, including Bismarck, who wished Prussia to take advantage of Austria's weakness in order to advance in Germany.

However, the dominant opinion within the government was that Prussia should support Austria, as a fellow German power, as a defender of the legitimate *status quo* and in order to contain the French threat. However, Prussia did wish to exact a price for such support, namely command of federal forces in the German theatre of war. This demand was intended not only to shift the balance of dualism towards Prussia. It was also based on a genuine fear that France might threaten not just in Italy but also in the Rhinelands. That, after all, was how the original Napoleon had proceeded. As it was, Austria was not prepared to pay this price at first. She fought alone in Italy and lost. She now found Prussia raising the price of cooperation even higher. This and other reasons led Austria rapidly to sue for peace with France in order to avoid the situation getting worse. Austria had clearly lost but equally Prussia had gained nothing. The dualist policy was at risk but no other policy had clearly emerged to take its place. The Prussian government was starting to assert rather more independence *vis-à-vis* Vienna by the time the 1859 war had finished but was not yet ready to openly challenge Austrian pre-eminence [13: *ch. 6*; 23, I: *150–2*; 24, I: *136–45*].

At home the king had been alarmed at the decrepit nature of the army revealed by the partial mobilisation that had been ordered in the crisis of 1859. As a consequence he sought to introduce radical reforms. First, he wished to call up a much higher proportion of those eligible for conscription. Second, he wanted to fix the term of service in the line regiments at three years and in the line reserves at five years, during which there would be a full training programme. Finally these men would serve eleven years in the reserve army, the *Landwehr*. This would bring about two radical changes. It would more than double the size of the regular army to 110,000. It would also greatly increase the size of the reserves as well. This was because the terms of service would be altered. Previously time in the line regiment had usually been two-and-a-half years, followed by two years in the line reserves and then fourteen years in the *Landwehr*. Furthermore, William and Roon, his Minister of War, now intended to relegate the *Landwehr* to garrison and rear-line duties, whereas it had had both a larger numerical and functional role in the unreformed army. To achieve all this required a massive increase in expenditure, the number of officers and of infantry and cavalry regiments. A bill to achieve this was introduced into the *Landtag* in February 1860 [36; 71: *136–48*].

The liberal majority in the *Landtag* had no objections to a strengthening of the army which they recognised was an essential instrument for a strong national policy. However, they did have qualms about the scale of the reforms both on financial and political grounds. There would be great increases in taxation. They were concerned that the army would not only become much stronger but would be a much more powerful weapon in the hands of the crown which could be used against internal opponents. Partly this was because they believed that the civic influence induced by a short full-time service and a powerful *Landwehr* presence would be eliminated by the reforms. Therefore the parliament would not go along with the full set of reforms and only provisionally granted monies for the programme. The king would not compromise. Repeated elections led to increased liberal majorities and the displacement of moderates by more determined liberals who formed the Progressive Party in early 1861. By the autumn of 1862 the situation had reached deadlock. William even hinted that he might abdicate. Instead Roon, who had summoned Bismarck back to Berlin, persuaded William to grant Bismarck an appointment with a view to appointing him Minister-President [71: *148–59*; 23, I: *ch. 5*; 24, I: *ch. 7*; 146: *113–18*; 16: *877–80*].

Otto von Bismarck, in September 1862 serving as Prussian ambassador to France, was no ordinary diplomat. Born in 1815 of a noble father and a bourgeois mother, he had studied at university with a civil service career in view. After graduation he began in the usual way as a probationary official. However, he soon abandoned this career and returned to run the family estates in Brandenburg. He had, apparently, turned his back upon the world of politics and power. (From the many studies of Bismarck see [23, I: *Pt I; 24*, I: *Bk 1*]. There is a hugely detailed consideration of the earlier part of Bismarck's life in Engelberg [183]: over 500 pages before his appointment as Minister President in 1862!)

It was the summoning of the United Diet in 1847 that brought him back into that world. He was elected a substitute to the Diet and ended up attending it. He soon made a name for himself as an extreme conservative defender of monarchical prerogative, although sometimes his cynical statements about what motivated people shocked his more principled conservative colleagues. In 1848 he turned up again in Berlin as a defender of the crown. From now on he was closely involved in the politics of the counter-revolution, usually advising that the most brutal and extreme methods for restoring order be employed in order to discourage any further attempts to overthrow the proper order of things. His view was that the great bulk of the population, especially in the countryside, had no sympathy for radicals and liberals, and would gladly fall behind their God-given rulers once those rulers had sufficient confidence to reassert their claims to power. (This is certainly the message of his reminiscences although they are unreliable and Bismarck often exaggerates.)

His reward for his part in the politics of royalist counter-revolution was his appointment as ambassador to the Diet of the restored *Bund* in 1851. It was an extraordinary decision as it meant Bismarck leapt over the ranks of career diplomats and courtiers. The modern politics of constitutionalism and revolution, even if Bismarck had set his face against them, had provided the jumping-off point for the career of this most unusual conservative.

In Frankfurt, where the Federal Diet met, Bismarck first encountered Austrian pre-eminence. This was a particularly galling moment for a patriotic and ambitious Prussian because Austria was still in the grip of the assertive policies of Schwarzenberg, even if the most ambitious objectives of that policy – the 70 million strong Confederation and *Zollverein* – had been abandoned. Whether Bismarck would have accepted a policy of dualism under the best of conditions is doubtful; under these circumstances Austria became his *bête noire* and a determination to destroy the *Bund* and all its works his major concern, indeed obsession.

This was amply demonstrated in the many memoranda with which he bombarded Berlin in these years. The consistent theme was to exploit Austrian weakness – during the Crimean war, then during the Italian war. Bismarck did not share the general conservative assumption that the maintenance of conservative rule at home entailed the defence of the *status quo* abroad, especially in Germany. His advice on exploiting Austria's involvement in war in Italy in 1859 produced one of his most striking and characteristically brutal statements that Prussia should:

march southwards with our entire army carrying frontier posts in our big packs. We can plant them either on the Bodensee or as far south as Protestantism is the dominant faith. [225, 14: doc.724, Bismarck to Gustav von Alvensleben, 23 April/5 May 1859]

54

Less remarked upon than the determination to destroy the existing pattern of dualism in Germany is Bismarck's qualification concerning Protestantism. He was always alive to the need to command the loyalty of subjects, even if that did not involve making them citizens of a parliamentary democracy. Increasingly from the later 1850s he also came to recognise that a forward policy for Prussia had to go beyond traditional dynastic justifications and include some appeal to the idea of nationality.

Bismarck's advice during the 1850s was unrealistic. Before 1854 Austria could depend upon Russian support. Prussia's army before the reforms started in 1861 was weak. The unconstitutional system of rule until 1858 meant that the government had little popular or middle-class support. Most national sentiment in 1859, both in and beyond Prussia, was pro-Austrian and anti-French. This was quite rational because between 1854 and 1860 French diplomatic and military performance was enjoying its greatest success under Napoleon III. One could excuse Bismarck on the grounds that he would have been less aware of these difficulties from his position in Frankfurt and perhaps would have put his anti-Austrian obsession into perspective if he had been charged with governmental responsibility in Berlin. What we certainly should not do is to assume that because his political calculations proved correct in the 1860s they would have also done so in the 1850s, or that his political success compels us to accept his own judgement in his tendentious and unreliable memoirs that a similar policy would have worked for Prussia earlier. (See, e.g. [226: *207–17, 221–7*] where he reflects upon Prussian politics from the turn of the century to his appointment as Minister-President and goes on to consider the relationship between dynastic and national loyalty [227, I: *298–312, 318–27*].)

Bismarck was moved to St Petersburg and the post of ambassador to Russia in 1859, partly to get him out of the way during the crisis caused by the Italian war where he dissented from the policies of Berlin. He was then appointed ambassador to France in January 1862, giving him a little time to study at close hand the character and rule of Louis-Napoleon, something which intrigued rather than offended him. In this he also differed from most Prussian conservatives, along with his willingness to contemplate agreements with the French ruler in order to advance Prussia's position in Germany [23, I: *131–41*; 24: *ch. 6*].

It was not his diplomatic opinions which led to Bismarck's

appointment as Minister-President in September 1862 but the domestic political crisis. Bismarck had always been a strong and courageous defender of royal prerogative and this was to be his role now. Although he had his doubts about William's intransigence on the military reform issue, in his interview with the king he declared his unswerving loyalty and his willingness to act as the king's servant in defiance of parliament. Indeed, in a way he made his appointment one of personal fealty rather than acceptance of a constitutional office, an emotional relationship which established a strong sense of obligation on the king's part and which Bismarck was often to use to his advantage in the future.

Bismarck, therefore, assumed power as the man who would rule in defiance of parliament. He was understandably preoccupied with this domestic crisis in his early months in office. One of his first steps was to withdraw the pending budget and to collect revenue under the budget approved for the previous year. He justified this on the basis of an argument known as the 'constitutional gap' theory. This stated that the constitution made no provision for the conduct of government in the event of a breakdown of the relationship between crown and parliament. However, it could not have been intended that government would at this point cease to operate at all. Therefore, in such a situation the executive must continue to govern the country on the basis of laws already passed. Needless to say, the parliamentary liberals rejected a constitutional argument which meant that their views could be ignored but Bismarck calculated rightly that they would never move beyond protest to a more effective method of resistance. During the period of the constitutional crisis Bismarck also sought to interfere with parliamentary immunity and began his distinguished career of trying to shape public opinion by harassing and bribing journalists and editors [23, I: *ch. 6*; 24, I: *ch. 9*].

In these circumstances it was difficult for Bismarck to pursue the assertive policy in Germany that he had previously advocated. It was not something which would command conservative support. When he tried to appeal to the liberals, in his notorious speech about a German policy having to be based on 'iron and blood' rather than parliamentary resolutions, this was seen as a threat to them rather than an offer to lead Prussia into Germany [23, I: *203–6*; 24, I: *179–84*]. Liberals assumed that he would not last long as he ruled against the most influential and progressive elements of society.

Conservatives at court watched him carefully for any signs of back-sliding. Early policy moves such as support for the Russian suppression of the Polish rising of 1863, although it helped secure Russian sympathy and neutrality in the future, simply enraged liberals as well as western European opinion generally. By the summer of 1863 Bismarck was confronted with an assertive German policy on the part of Austria and had to use all his powers of persuasion and personality and even emotional blackmail to prevent William attending the Princes' Congress in August 1863.

By the autumn of 1863 the constitutional crisis remained unresolved; Bismarck's major diplomatic achievement was an anti-Polish agreement with Russia; in Germany it was proving difficult to sustain a policy of dualism against Austria, let alone to go on the offensive. Bismarck might want to break out of this cage but he did not seem to have a key with which to unpick the lock.

That key was provided with the onset of the Schleswig-Holstein crisis in November 1863. In retrospect we can see that as the moment when the process of unification began.

3 Processes

The German state was formed by a process of politics and war and that is what I will focus upon in this chapter, although economic and cultural matters will be introduced when relevant. I will continue to look at events on the four levels of Europe, Germany, Austria and Prussia, in each case considering three phases: the origins, pattern and outcome of the wars between Germany and Denmark, Austria and Prussia, and France and Germany. (In the last phase France replaces Austria in the account.)

[i] The war between Germany and Denmark

[a] Introduction

The affairs of Schleswig-Holstein had already caused an international crisis in 1848–9 leading to a brief war between Germany (notably Prussia) and Denmark. The issues were temporarily resolved by international negotiations resulting in the Treaty of London in 1852.

Schleswig and Holstein were two duchies ruled by the Danish crown but on different terms from those on which Denmark proper was ruled. The population of Holstein was German-speaking and Holstein was a member of the German Confederation. A large part of the population of Schleswig, especially in its southern and central districts, were German-speaking but there was also a Danish-speaking population in the central and northern districts. The German speakers included the leading social groups of the duchy and dominated the estates-government there as well as in Holstein.

The major political questions were the indivisibility of the two duchies and the terms on which the Danish crown ruled. The intensification of national feeling in Denmark as well as in Germany made it increasingly difficult to resolve this problem. Danish nationalists claimed Schleswig as Danish and wished to see it ruled on the same basis as the rest of Denmark. German nationalists claimed that the two Duchies belonged together and should be part of the German Confederation. The law of succession was different for Denmark and the Duchies. When Frederick VII died on 15 November 1863 his designated successor to the Danish crown, Christian IX, could not succeed to rule in the Duchies because there inheritance proceeded only through the male line. Before Frederick died the Danish parliament and government drew up a charter (the March Charter) which would effectively have incorporated Schleswig into the Danish kingdom. On this basis a constitution was drawn up. Frederick, who was dying, did not sign the constitution but Christian did shortly after acceding to the Danish throne ([64] for background; [20] for the war; [25] for details of diplomacy).

At this point German nationalist sentiment exploded and insisted that the title of Duke of Schleswig-Holstein should be granted to Frederick, Duke of Augustenberg, who would bring both Duchies into the German Confederation.

[b] Europe

As the dispute was already regulated by international treaty the major powers were entitled to take a view on it. This was also a matter of some concern to Britain and Russia because the area was important for trade between the Baltic and the North Sea. France was less immediately affected but was interested in anything which could destabilise other states.

Generally the major powers took a similar position. They had no time for the national demands of either the Danes or the Germans, both of which were in contravention of the Treaty of London. Their main concern was to put pressure on both sides to return to that treaty, seeking to preserve a connection between Denmark and the Duchies but at the same time ensuring that the Danish crown respect the rights and autonomies of the Duchies. The powers were relieved, therefore, when Austria and Prussia signified that they too wished to proceed in this way. Increasingly it appeared to the major powers that it was the Danish who were blocking the way [21: *chs 6 & 7*].

59

The Danish position was complicated by the internal situation. There was a strong national movement which wanted to incorporate Schleswig into the Danish kingdom, even at the expense of giving up any connection with Holstein. This was broadly the policy pursued by the Danish Minister-President, Carl Christian Hall, during the crisis. Hall was constrained by strong public opinion and support from the national liberals who took up this *Eiderdan* position. (*Eiderdan* means extending Denmark to the river Dan, i.e. incorporating the whole of Schleswig.) Hall tried to pursue a conciliatory line for as long as possible, in particular making generous concessions to Holstein, partly to try to distance it from the Germans in Schleswig. Danish policy was conditioned by the persistent belief that the major powers, as well as Sweden, would not allow German military action to detach Schleswig from Denmark.

With the refusal of the Danish crown to withdraw the November constitution and return to the agreements of 1851–2 (these included promises to consult the estates of the Duchies on modes of government as well as observing the terms of the Treaty of London), the Federal Diet insisted on taking action to protect Holstein. In late 1863 Saxon and Hannoverian soldiers, acting for the *Bund*, occupied Holstein. Denmark still refused to negotiate.

British policy was undecided. There was a natural concern to stand by Denmark as the smaller power but there were also elements – for example, in the royal court – which favoured the Augustenberg cause. In any case, the British had little sympathy when the Danish took an intransigent line, especially when they refused to consider a partition of Schleswig, which, in the British view, would have provided a neat and national solution to the problem. However, although Palmerston was prepared to take strong action in support of Denmark if Augustenberg was established Duke of Schleswig-Holstein, it soon became clear that Britain would not act alone. Britain had other concerns worldwide and needed a continental ally if she was to act decisively. Palmerston contemplated going further unilaterally but was overruled by the whole cabinet [20: *78 9*; 21: *ch. 6*]. British policy in relation to Schleswig-Holstein from then on was either one of 'pure bluff' [53: *107*] or quite clear non-intervention.

The French were not prepared to support Denmark because Louis-Napoleon hoped to gain something out of such international complications and in any case favoured some kind of a national solution to the issue. Russia was broadly pro-Danish but also disapproved of the more radical and nationalist elements making policy in Copenhagen and was in any case concerned to maintain good relations with Austria and Prussia as she dealt with the aftermath of the Polish insurrection of 1863 [21: *ch. 6*].

What this meant was that there was no concerted international action when Austrian and Prussian troops invaded Schleswig at the end of January 1864, especially as the two powers pointed out that they were doing this in defence of the Treaty of London, that they were not disputing Danish rights in Schleswig and Holstein and that they were not acting in support of the Augustenberg claim.

The superior Austro-Prussian forces soon secured control in Schleswig. International pressure led to an armistice which ran from April to June, during which the various parties met in London to see if a negotiated solution could be found. The failure of the Danish to offer any clear compromise proposal, such as partition of Schleswig, lost them international sympathy. Denmark also rejected the proposal for purely Personal Union because in her view this would abandon the Danes of Schleswig to German domination as there would be no chance of altering the local form of government. However, this refusal now left the way open for Austria and Prussia to declare in favour of the Augustenberg candidacy. Denmark continued to hope for international intervention. It did not come and war resumed in June [20: *81–4*; 13: *146–54*].

It is not necessary to enter into the military details because there was little doubt that the Austrian and Prussian forces were superior to those of Denmark [20: *84–5*; 71: *181–92*]. Denmark did miscalculate her defensive capacities which perhaps in turn explains faulty diplomacy. With Schleswig conquered and Denmark herself threatened with invasion, she soon accepted defeat, giving over the two Duchies to Austria and Prussia in October 1864. From now on the disposition of the Duchies was a matter for Austria and Prussia alone. The issue of European intervention would arise again only in the event of conflict between those two powers [21: *ch. 7*].

There was a longer-term military consequence. Austrian troops did well in the war and Prussian soldiers only distinguished themselves in the last major action. This could encourage Austrian optimism about a war with Prussia. At the same time the Prussian army had an opportunity to put its new, as yet untried reforms, into practice. Finally, the conduct of the war convinced Wilhelm of the need to move Moltke, the chief of the general staff, into what was effectively the position of supreme commander. The war planner rather than the distinguished battlefield general or the head of state was in charge, unlike in Austria and France respectively.

[c] Germany

Part of the reason the major powers did not resist Austro-Prussian action in Schleswig-Holstein was because it appeared much more moderate than the position taken by the other German states and national opinion. The Federal Diet, the *kleindeutsch National Verein* and the *großdeutsch Reform Verein* were united in supporting the Augustenberg candidacy. There was great indignation when Austria and Prussia declared that they would act independently of the Diet and were seeking only to compel Denmark to return to the Treaty of London. When Austrian and Prussian troops moved through Holstein to invade Schleswig, they encountered sullen attitudes amongst the other German troops who had occupied Holstein as a *Bund* military force.

This national opinion was not confined to northern Germany. The wave of pro-Augustenberg demonstrations was perhaps strongest in south-west Germany and the Municipal Council of Vienna petitioned the Emperor on behalf of the Augustenberg cause. For a period the *großdeutsch Reform Verein* and the *kleindeutsch National Verein* were at one; if anything it was the *National Verein* which had the most difficulty because of the anti-national line pursued by Bismarck ([16: *895–9*; 97; 201: *ch. 7*; 158: *ch. 9*; 144: *153–5*; 90 & 166] for biographical details of two very different liberals).

There was a brief outburst of rather astonished jubilation when Austria and Prussia declared in favour of the Augustenberg cause in May 1864. It was expected that once Denmark had given up control in the Duchies the next step would be to create the Duchy of Schleswig-Holstein under Augustenberg rule. Instead the two Duchies were subjected to a *de facto* military occupation by the two German powers. Prussia set conditions for supporting the Augustenberg claim which Augustenberg could not accept (or perhaps, which the Austrians would not allow him to accept) because it so effectively established Prussian control over the new state. Little of these negotiations were known about by the national movement or the smaller states. All they knew was that 'Germany' now controlled the Duchies but a 'German' solution, namely the incorporation of Schleswig-Holstein into the German Confederation as a new state, was not taking place.

Hardly any of the other German states or the national movement were happy with this. Austro-Prussian tension in the Duchies was temporarily removed with the Gastein Convention of August 1865. This created two military occupation zones: Holstein under Austria and Schleswig under Prussia. The national movement could only rail impotently at this brutal, non-national settlement [158: *363–70*]. There were, however, some elements of national liberalism, especially in Prussia, which had now come round to the prospect of Schleswig and Holstein falling under Prussian rule [201: *esp. 213–23*; 158: *356–70*]. But as yet this was a minority view and in any case Austria still stood in the way of such an outcome.

[d] Austria

Austria had no interest in Schleswig-Holstein except for her general responsibility for German affairs. Already in the early 1850s she had acted jointly with Prussia and independently of the *Bund* to re-establish order in Schleswig-Holstein. Given her opposition to the national movement and her own interest in defending international treaties, Austria was happy to pursue a dualist policy with Prussia. Her problem was how to prevent this dualism working to Prussia's advantage, given that Schleswig-Holstein was geographically adjacent to Prussian territory but far from Austria.

In early 1864 Austria tried to bind Prussia to acceptance of the Treaty of London as the basis of settlement because this had been the original justification of their joint action. This failed. As the chances of pursuing any 'Danish option' declined, so Austria found herself locked into involvement with a province far away from her own territories or interests. In 1865 she took up the Augustenberg cause, although this was never pushed consistently or resolutely against Prussa. It was somewhat ironic when the Prussian government declared that agitation for the Augustenbergs was treasonable.

Given this story, Austria has often been portrayed as a dupe of Bismarck's policy in the period 1863–5. However, it is a good working rule for an historian to try to explain behaviour as rational in the given circumstances before reaching such a conclusion. As has already been argued, Austria could defend her position in Germany either with or against Prussia. Most of the time she preferred the

63

dualist policy. Earlier in 1863, when Schmerling was the major determinant of policy, the alternative ideas of federal reform and bringing together the German princes had been pursued, but this all fell to the ground as soon as Prussia refused to go along with the policy and as the different states also backed away from any genuine reform proposals. By late 1863 policymakers in Austria, led now by the Foreign Minister Rechberg, were happy to return to the dualist policy. (For Austrian policy in 1863–4 see [48: *133–6*; 4: *ch. 3*; 218; 101; 22: *74–7*; 79; 5].)

There were very great advantages to be had from such a policy. The national movement was feared as potentially radical. If dualist action with Prussia cut Austria off from support from the other German states and the national movement, it also had the same effect on Prussia. To act with Prussia in defence of international treaty obligations was desirable, even if one could not quite pin Prussia down to accepting that the Duchies could only be separated from Denmark by mutual agreement between Austria and Prussia [4: *50*].

Once the Danish government had blocked any possible agreement, then Austria had little option but to move towards support of the Augustenberg candidacy. The problem was that she could not control the conditions that the Prussians would set in their support for this candidacy by virtue of her regional influence and interests. When such conditions proved unacceptable, Austria continued the dualist policy in the form of occupation. But clearly this policy was under strain as Austria sought unsuccessfully to gain concessions, under the principles of dualism, from Prussia in other matters such as the *Zollverein* issue or support in Italy. Rechberg, the architect of the dualist policy, was forced to resign in October 1864 in the light of this failure.

Austria then attempted to move towards a more assertive policy, above all by rejecting the onerous conditions Prussia tied to acceptance of the Augustenberg claim. The only leverage she had was to push this policy forward in Holstein against Prussian resistance. This Austria did in early 1865. By May 1865 war seemed likely as a consequence. However, in both capitals there were those advocating a settlement. Schmerling fell from office in July 1865, clearing the way for a policy of reconciliation with Prussia. Indeed, the Gastein Convention of August 1865 – which at least delayed war with Prussia – was the last expression of the dualist policy. The Convention, and Austria in particular as the state which had up until now pushed the Augustenberg cause, were bitterly denounced by German nationalists.

In considering Austrian policy one must also relate it to the internal situation of the empire. The fall of Schmerling was due to the failure of his attempt at centralised yet constitutional government in the empire as a whole. The constitution Schmerling had introduced in February 1861 was abolished in September 1865. Those who replaced Schmerling sought to move towards more aristocratic and church influence in the western half of the empire. In the eastern half they were compelled to give ground to the Hungarian demands for greater autonomy [16: *893–5*; 48: *120–36*; 118: *539–60*; 104, II: *125–33*].

One could see an ominous significance in this. Settlement of Hungarian demands created greater freedom to act in Germany. From now on Austrian concern was not to lose out to Prussia in Schleswig-Holstein. Schemes were floated of selling Holstein to Prussia (just as similar schemes for selling Venetia to Italy were suggested) but to have accepted such schemes would have been to signal the end of Austrian pre-eminence in Germany. There were many in Vienna who still wished to maintain dualism with Prussia but not at any price. Everything therefore depended on what Prussia wanted.

[e] Prussia

This is the best known part of the story. Bismarck claimed that the way he handled the Schleswig-Holstein affair was the greatest of all his diplomatic achievements and many historians have concurred. (Generally for Bismarck's policies see [23, I: *ch. 7*; 24, I: *ch. 11*; ibid., p. *242*] for Bismarck's claim.)

It is doubtful whether Bismarck had a clear objective when the crisis broke in November 1863. Clearly it provided an opportunity for a forward foreign policy. However, Bismarck had no wish to alienate other powers. His first concern, therefore, was to act in defence of international treaty obligations. This may have dismayed the national movement and the Federal Diet but it created a legitimate diplomatic ground for action and could be used to gain Austrian cooperation.

Once troops were in occupation Bismarck was confident that he could control the situation and now could contemplate his preferred option: annexation of the Duchies to Prussia. First, war with Denmark removed any treaty obligations Prussia and Austria had with her. Second, by avoiding any clear commitment to Austria that the connection of the Duchies with Denmark could only be severed by mutual consent, and also by introducing as a condition of continued Danish rule her agreement to abide by various promises made in 1851–2 as to how the Duchies were to be governed, Bismarck created the justification for his claim that Denmark was not fulfilling conditions that would enable her to continue to govern in the Duchies.

At the peace table in London Bismarck had other cards to play. He had to go along with the idea of Personal Union with Denmark but was helped out of that difficulty by the Danish refusal to accept it. He also could point to the continuation of German national enthusiasm (which at this time he was happy to encourage) as something which had to be taken into account in any settlement. If Denmark had accepted the partition option Bismarck might well have had further difficulties, but again Danish adamancy on this let him off that hook.

Bismarck now had to go along with the Augustenberg movement to some extent. However, he made it clear that a Schleswig-Holstein under Augustenberg rule would have to join Prussia's military system, allow her to operate naval bases and build a canal across its territory, and become a member of the *Zollverein*. Augustenberg might have been prepared to accept those conditions but Austria could not.

Once Denmark had been forced out and Austrian and Prussian troops occupied the Duchies, Bismarck was content to wait. When later on the Austrians asked when a final settlement would be made in the Duchies, Bismarck replied that he was quite happy for the present military occupation arrangements to continue indefinitely.

It did appear in early 1865, however, that Bismarck was prepared to go to war with Austria to block her attempts to push the Augustenberg candidacy. A number of reasons have been suggested for why this did not happen. There was still a powerful peace party in Berlin, including the Crown Prince, who believed in the policy of dualism. William himself required much persuasion to break the old alliance with Austria, an alliance he had first experienced as a young man in 1813 when it was directed against Napoleon. There were problems in raising sufficient monies to finance a war at this time, especially given the continuing constitutional crisis which made it difficult to raise extra revenues. No agreement with Italy had yet been negotiated which would weaken Austria by opening up the prospect of a two-front war. So the decision was put off. But Bismarck had already made it clear that he was set upon ending dualism in Germany and to do that was prepared to go to war with Austria [20: *122–5*].

[ii] The Austro-Prussian war

[a] Europe

Generally speaking the same points that have been made about British and Russian policy in the Schleswig-Holstein crisis apply to the Austro-Prussian crisis as well. Britain clearly had no wish to see war in central Europe but was not prepared to intervene if such a war did break out. In any case, there were those in the government and the court, as well as represented in public opinion, who sympathised with some national solution. Generally, however, this sympathy was with a liberal Prussian policy, not with the policies of Bismarck. Furthermore, Britain was far more concerned about France than the German powers. Since the end of the Crimean war relations with the French had deteriorated markedly. The war with Austria in 1859 had produced France's first territorial gains in Europe since Napoleon's time. France had advocated intervention in support of the Polish insurrection of 1863. The British government had come under some pressure from pro-Polish public opinion but had stuck to its non-interventionist posture. The matter had soured relations between the two countries. The main concern of the British was that France might derive some advantage from a war in Germany rather than what that would mean for Germany itself. Queen Victoria mooted more interventionist policies but such initiatives were resisted by her government [21: *ch. 8*; 53: *107–10*]. Both Austria and Prussia could assume that Britain would do nothing unless and until it appeared that the French might gain something by intervening in an Austro-Prussian conflict.

Russia also was less preoccupied with central European affairs after the end of the Crimean war. The war had clearly revealed that her armies could no longer dominate even in her own territories, let alone in other parts of Europe. Financial and political crisis induced a turn to domestic preoccupations – either reform (the peasant emancipation measure of 1861) or repression (the Polish insurrection of 1863). If there was a forward foreign policy it was to be found either in the Far East (leading to conflict with Britain) or manipulating crises in the Ottoman Empire (to which only Prussia, of the major powers, had no objection). The legacy of Austrian policy from the Crimean war still poisoned relations between the two countries, whereas Prussia's more muted policies at the time meant that she had incurred less Russian disapproval. Prussian support for Russia in the face of the Polish insurrection of 1863 had also improved their relations. Nevertheless, Russia was concerned about the expansion of Prussian power, especially given the radical proposals for German reform Bismarck had made. In 1866, therefore, Russia favoured Austrian victory [21: *238–9*]. (Taylor [13: *166–9*] asserts that Russia favoured Prussia but, unlike Mosse [21], provides no supporting evidence. I accept Mosse's view.) However, she was not prepared to intervene to help secure this or to prevent Prussian success. Neither Austria nor Prussia could expect much involvement from Britain or Russia in the event of their going to war with each other [21: *ch. 8*; 13: *156–7* for the general import of this].

The major power whose policies were of concern was France. Napoleon III was the unpredictable factor in European diplomacy. His policies had proved highly successful through the 1850s; they were less so in the first half of the 1860s. Failing health and the fiasco in Mexico made him less formidable but also more concerned to renew foreign policy successes ([119: *ch. 5*] for domestic context; [137] for diplomacy).

Napoleon regarded the dualist policy of Austria and Prussia with hostility. As long as the two major powers to the east of France agreed with one another, with Austria supporting Prussia in Germany and Prussia supporting Austria in Italy, then there was little opportunity for France to bring about change and extend her own influence. He was, therefore, happy to see tensions develop between Austria and Prussia and to try to work out how France could gain from this. This had partly been his calculation with the Schleswig-Holstein affair but by late 1864 France had achieved nothing from this. As tensions mounted in the summer of 1865 the issue of French policy once more became significant.

In October Bismarck met with Napoleon at Biarritz. Napoleon was not prepared to make any firm commitments. He was happy to see tension rise in Germany and to remain fairly free to act according to how things developed. However, this was not a completely even-handed, opportunist policy. Napoleon did find it difficult to cooperate with Austria, a conservative dynasty committed to maintenance of the *status quo*. His own pro-national position meant that he tended to favour an extension of Prussian influence in northern Germany. He was also concerned to 'complete' his pro-Italian policy which also tended France to an anti-Austrian position. However, this was balanced by a concern to ensure that Prussia did not extend her territory and influence by too much and to this end he favoured some enlargement of the medium German states to act as a counter-weight. Finally, if France could make some direct gains from an Austro-Prussian confrontation, Napoleon was not averse to that but was unclear as to what form these might take. There were vague mentions of Belgium but that would offend Britain. The problem with Rhinelands territory was that it could offend German national feeling and went against Napoleon's own pro-national pronouncements. Later Luxemburg would appear as the best prospect. Generally one can see Napoleon's policy as similar to Bismarck's: no clear or specific objectives, just a readiness to profit when circumstances were ripe. All France could do was help the ripening process. It also meant that no other government could easily predict French policy. Bismarck was coming to be regarded with suspicion by men of principle – liberal or conservative – but Napoleon aroused the greater concerns given his track record of achievements and the greater power of France compared to Prussia.

It was through Italy that Napoleon found a way forward. The major objective of the Italian government was to complete the unification of Italy. Two things remained to be achieved: the recovery of Venetia and Venice from Austrian rule and the removal of Papal authority in Rome. The Papacy was backed by French soldiers and this objective had to be placed on hold, so the acquisition of Venetia was given priority [91: *243–4*; 13: *158–61*].

The Italians, therefore, had a similar interest to France in there being tension between Austria and Prussia. Just as Prussia wished to use the Italian threat as a weapon against Austria, so the Italians wished to do precisely the same with the Prussian threat. Even to begin negotiations would compel Austria to move towards either concessions or war. By early 1866 Italy was ready to explore links with Prussia. In March, as tension mounted over Schleswig-Holstein, General Govone arrived in Berlin. The problem was that these negotiations were marked by intense mutual distrust. Each side assumed that the other would prefer to force concessions from Austria without resorting to war. Both sides, therefore, were anxious that they did not find themselves the victim of this process; that Prussia did not find that Austria had conceded in Italy in order the better to defend her German position, and that Italy did not find Austria conceding in Germany in order the better to defend her Italian position.

It was Napoleon who, wishing to foment Austro-Prussian tension, provided the support necessary to bring the Italians to an agreement with Prussia. Under the terms of this agreement, which was restricted to a period of just three months, Italy agreed to go to war with Austria if Prussia did. Prussia did not make the same commitment. On the other hand, once war did break out both parties agreed not to make peace until each had obtained territorial gains – Venetia for Italy, some undefined equivalent for Prussia. This put pressure on Prussia to act quickly in order to profit from this military alliance.

As for the position of Napoleon, it can be best summed up in the report of a conversation at this time in which he was supposed to have said:

In this way [by means of the Prussian-Italian agreement] Italy will get Venice, and France will benefit by the conflict of the two powers whose alliance hems her in. Once the struggle has begun France can throw her weight into the balance and must obviously become arbitrator and master of the situation. By occupying the Rhineland with 100,000 men I should be able to dictate the terms of peace. [4: *113–14*]

Napoleon also, very shortly before the war broke out, was engaged in discussions with Austria. As with Prussia, objectives remained unclear. There were vague references to Austrian gains in Germany, accompanied by some verbal points concerning a strengthening of the medium states at the expense of the smaller ones and an independent Rhineland state. A constant feature of French policy was the idea of strengthening the medium states such as Bavaria and Württemberg. The advantage was clear: in this way if either Austrian or Prussian power was drastically weakened in Germany powerful bulwarks would still remain against the complete dominance of the victorious power. However, only one element in the agreement was clear: Austria would cede Venetia to Italy. Defence of her German position took priority over her Italian position. Italy stood to gain whichever way the war ended. Whether she could therefore have obtained Venetia without war is debatable.

In certain respects it was Italian action which brought the final crisis to a head. The Austrians began mobilising troops in Bohemia in late April. This led to a flurry of talks between Austria and Prussia in which those in the respective governments who wanted to avoid war made a last effort to defuse the situation. At this point the Italians began mobilising their army, calling up fresh troops and transferring soldiers from the south of Italy. The Austrians had no choice but to mobilise in response, insisting that they were only doing this with respect to the Army of the South. But it was easy for the war party in Berlin, headed by Bismarck, to say one could not discriminate between one and another purpose of mobilisation. Faced with this argument William felt he had little choice but to order Prussian mobilisation in the first days of May [26: *ch. 2*].

[b] Germany

Germany was the victim rather than the subject of the war of 1866. (Sheehan entitles his account of this 'The German Civil War' [16: *899–911*].) Except for brief moments since November 1863 Austria and Prussia had acted together independently of or even against the other German states and the national movement. Both governments appealed to Germans elsewhere but such appeals took the form of declamatory notes accusing the rival power of pursuing anti-German policies. There was little attempt by either government actually to obtain the approval of the Federal Diet or to bring organisations such as the *National Verein* or the *Reform Verein* over to their side. Austria did take up the Augustenberg cause again in early 1865 but mainly as a weapon against Prussia and then promptly deserted the German cause with the Gastein Convention of 1865. The war of 1866 was a cabinet war: there was no significant popular pressure upon either government to go to war.

The national movement was in a dilemma. Whether *kleindeutsch* or *großdeutsch*, liberal or radical, it was opposed to war between the two major German powers. Naturally conservatives opposed war [201: *224–6*; 97; 228: *61–4*; 158: *385–402*]. Public opinion tacked back and forth according to whether it held one or the other power more responsible for pushing events towards war. When war actually

71

broke out state loyalty tended to prevail amongst the Austrian and Prussian supporters of national unity and others remained divided. A minority of *National Verein* members did shift towards support of Prussian policy but the effect was to divide the organisation and reduce its influence [97: *ch. 6*; 158; 146: *117–19*; 16: *900–1, 906–7*].

The individual states also watched helplessly. The medium states, with the exception of Baden, considered that their own relative independence depended upon continued Austro-Prussian dualism. If dualism degenerated into war then most of these states would tend to support Austria. Austria could envisage beating Prussia and reducing her power within Germany but never actually excluding her from Germany and destroying all traces of dualism and federalism. That was not the case with Prussia. She directly threatened the independence of the largely Protestant states of northern and central Germany. In addition, in south German states with large Catholic populations there was strong public pressure behind a pro-Austrian stance.

One can see this at work in the response of Bavaria to a vague approach from Prussia in the summer of 1866. Probably the approach was never seriously intended; rather it could serve to display to France that Prussia did not seek simple hegemony in Germany. Nevertheless the Bavarian government reacted with an uncompromising rejection. Hannover and Electoral Hesse responded in the same way to intense pressure from Prussia on the eve of war.

In very instrumental ways both Prussia and Austria tried to play the national card as the crisis reached its climax. Austria had once more taken up the Augustenberg cause in late 1865 and it was to be Prussian insistence that Austria cease permitting pro-Augustenberg demonstrations in Holstein which sparked off the final crisis. However, Austria did not go on to develop a broader, principled national programme on which to mobilise support in the rest of Germany. Prussia in the spring of 1866 also bid for national support by outlining a plan for reform of the Confederation which included the calling of a national parliament elected on the basis of universal manhood suffrage [24, I: *303–8*].

In terms of the choices made by German nationalists and states in June 1866 when war finally broke out, neither of these 'national' policies made much impact. It was recognised that the war was about great power interests, not national objectives. The Prussian plan in particular was greeted with cynicism. Here was a government which ruled roughshod over its own parliament – practising censorship and seeking to bully deputies into compliance – which now expected the German public to take seriously its commitment to a democratic parliament playing a major role in political life if it beat Austria in war [158: *385–94*].

When finally in June 1866 the Federal Diet had to take sides, the decision was made in terms of existing state interest. Most of the medium states – Hannover, Saxony, Württemberg, Electoral Hesse, Hesse-Darmstadt, Bavaria – voted for the Austrian motion to mobilise non-Prussian Federal troops behind the Federal (i.e. the Austrian) cause. Smaller states in northern Germany which dared not offend their powerful neighbour – the Mecklenburg states, Oldenburg, the three Hanseatic city-states of Hamburg, Lübeck and Bremen – voted against the motion. Baden, pro-Prussian but in southern Germany, abstained. The leaders of the national movement condemned both governments for betraying the German interest by plunging the country into a civil war which could only ravage and weaken it and provide foreigners with great opportunities to profit at Germany's expense.

[c] Austria

Austrian policy continued to display the same oscillation between seeking dualism and domination in Germany, although with Schmerling's departure it was the dualist position which tended to prevail. From late 1865 when Austria once more took up the Augustenberg cause she did not, as Schmerling might well have done, use this to mobilise national feeling and to generate support amongst the other German states. Rather it was used as a weapon to try to bring Prussia to some settlement. The Austrian government intimated that they would consider abandoning the Augustenberg cause and ceding Prussian control in Schleswig-Holstein but only at a price. That price was most likely support for regaining lost territory in Italy. The problem was that Prussia was not prepared to fight in Italy (or rather, to mobilise against France) in order to gain Schleswig-Holstein. The Austrians lacked any leverage with which they could compel Prussia to come to some agreement. On the other hand, Austria did not feel that she could continue indefinitely in the military occupation of the Duchies, where she was always subject to the pressures that Prussia as the neighbouring power could bring to bear whenever she wished.

The only choices, therefore, were either to give way to Prussia in Schleswig-Holstein (receiving payment for Holstein would have been such a policy) or to compel Prussia to give way in turn. Austria never seriously contemplated the former policy (though pessimistic dualists sometimes commended it). Retreat from Germany, following in the wake of retreat from Italy, would have signalled the end of Austria's claim to be a major European power. One can see this in the terms in which Austria, in February 1863, had rejected the idea floated by Bismarck that she consider Buda-Pest the centre of her empire.

If Berlin makes us choose between withdrawing from Germany – moving, as the Prussian Minister suggests, our centre of gravity to Buda-Pest – and the threat of finding Prussia among our enemies in the next European conflict, we must leave such ideas to the judgement of public opinion; and it will decisively condemn them, should they ever be put into practice. [Austrian note to German courts, 28 February 1863. Quoted in 4: *34–5*.]

That left Austria with the policy of compelling Prussia to give way. Such a policy was difficult to reconcile with the maintenance of dualism, yet Austria persisted in seeing things in these terms. Threat of war, even war itself, was a way of preventing Prussia acquiring dominance in Germany rather than of reconstructing Germany along new lines. With aristocratic, cosmopolitan ministers like Esterhazy shaping policy in Vienna in 1866 it is understandable why the confrontation with Prussia was not accompanied by any national programme or ideas of establishing Austrian hegemony. In any case, such Austrian ministers did not believe that Prussia would ultimately take the awful risk of war. They remembered Olmütz and were aware that William himself had grave doubts about war and that there were influential voices in Berlin counselling agreement with Austria. Whatever the case, as the crisis approached its climax, Austria signalled that her German position mattered more than even that of Italy and agreed with France to the cession of Venetia in return for a free hand in settling German affairs once Prussia had been beaten [21: *ch. 8*; 48: *136–9*; 69; 101; 218; 13; 22: *79–83*].

Austria did not assume that she would lose the war. Nor did most contemporaries. Austria had lost in 1859 but her troops had fought well and she had withdrawn from the war as much because of problems elsewhere as for what had happened on the battlefields of northern Italy. In the war against Denmark in 1864 Austrian soldiers had fought bravely and effectively and indeed had impressed some observers much more than the Prussian army. Austrian policymakers were aware of certain weaknesses, for example, in the ability to mobilise and move troops quickly but these were not regarded as sufficient to make them pessimistic [see documents in 2: *155–63*].

By contrast Prussia had last engaged in a major war in 1813–15. She had been sufficiently worried about her military capability to plunge the country into a constitutional crisis over army reforms in the early 1860s. The results of those reforms had not yet been put to a serious test. Austria could depend upon the support of the other German states with a significant military force – principally Bavaria, Hannover, Electoral Hesse and Saxony. Until war actually broke out Prussia could not move her troops into central and southern Germany whereas Bohemia pressed upwards into Prussia, a good place to defend but also a possible jumping-off point for a strike towards either Berlin or Silesia.

The Austrians did face serious problems. There was the Italian mobilisation which would compel them to fight a war on two fronts. Endemic financial crisis had stymied various measures of military modernisation. Austria had considered changing over to the needle-gun, the rapid-fire rifle with which Prussian troops were equipped in 1866, but had not done so and financial concerns might well have been part of the reason for this. Military expenditure was cut by virtually 50 per cent between 1861 and 1865, just as it was sharply rising in Prussia. Austria had reverted to the doctrine of close engagement of infantry and the use of the bayonet but that might be considered a rationale for not spending money on expensive re-equipping of her infantry. However, she did have good artillery.

There had been no effective war planning with Bavaria, Hannover, Hesse and Saxony: one consequence of the dualist policy pursued by Austria up to 1866. Austria faced difficulties in mobilising her army against Prussia. Only one railway line ran from Vienna to Bohemia, the place where it was generally agreed the first decisive battles would come, and even that was single-track for much of its length. Prussia on the other hand could call upon five lines for bringing her soldiers and equipment southwards. Austria would have to mobilise much earlier or delay battle for much longer if she was to overcome this handicap. Also, it is here that the multinational character of the Habsburg army caused considerable weakness. Austria had a policy of not stationing troops near to their homes, for fear of desertion and because they would be unreliable in dealing with domestic unrest. As a consequence troops were far more widely dispersed than was the case in Prussia. Whether this made any difference to what happened on the battlefield is much harder to judge. Certainly many Habsburg soldiers, of different nationalities, fought with great courage in the war of 1866. (On the military background from the Austrian point of view see [26: *ch. 1*; 77: *esp. 48–53*; 148: *Pt I*].)

For these reasons Austria continued, while refusing to back down, to hope that confrontation would not lead to war. As late as 7 April 1866 she sent a note to Prussia offering a peaceful resolution of the issues. Peace party elements in Berlin managed to get a conciliatory reply sent to this note on 15 April. At that point, however, came the Italian mobilisation. The military planners in Vienna overruled the politicians, an indication of the new pressures created by the capacity to mobilise and move very large numbers of soldiers, above all by rail. The moment for peaceful negotiation passed. Bismarck was back in control of policy in Prussia. War came when all three states mobilised their troops in early May.

[d] Prussia

If Bismarck planned any war, it was the war against Austria. His consistent view since the 1850s had been that dualism was untenable; there must be a clear division of Germany between a sphere of Prussian and a sphere of Austrian influence. At times he indicated that he hoped this could be worked out without resort to war but it was clear, if Austria was not prepared to move in this direction, then the threat of war, and if necessary, war itself must be used to compel that outcome. The Schleswig-Holstein affair had provided a welcome opportunity for Prussia to develop a more forward foreign policy but it could not be converted into a clear Prussian success without that confrontation with Austria. Consequently, his policy from October 1864, when Denmark ceded her rights in Schleswig-Holstein, makes most sense seen as a strategy for pushing Austria out of north and central Germany. Schleswig-Holstein itself offered numerous opportunities for pursuing this policy but only when other conditions had been met. (For a detailed account of Bismarck's motives and policies see [23, I: *ch. 8*; 24, I: *ch. 13*; 20: *ch. 3*].)

The first condition was to isolate any crisis and war from external interference. As we have seen this was not really a problem so far as Britain and Russia were concerned [21: *ch. 8*]. More difficult were the positions of France and Italy. We have already considered things from their point of view. Many accounts present Napoleon as a dupe of Bismarck – misled into inaction by vague promises of territorial gains in areas such as Luxembourg. Yet this judgement is made only in the light of the rapid Prussian victory over Austria. Any other result – either an Austrian victory or a prolonged war – would have vindicated French policy. Only if one assumes that the military outcome was just about inevitable and that Bismarck knew this (and perhaps Napoleon should have known it), would this judgement be reasonable. Yet hardly anyone took that view at the time. A few years earlier, even the Prussian army command did not take that view. These are the judgements of Moltke, Chief of General Staff in the Prussian army, in 1860:

> If there is a break between Austria and Prussia the struggle will produce a strong empire under Habsburg or Hohenzollern; but Germany will have to pay for her unification with the loss of provinces in the east and the west. [Minute of February 1860, quoted in 4: *33–4*.]

> The German nation of seventy million people which would emerge from the struggle [between Austria and Prussia] would certainly be an unwelcome result for France, but she can count on tremendous gains – the annexation of Belgium, the Rhine provinces, and perhaps Holland – while the Prussian forces are engaged on the Elbe and the Oder. [Quoted in 4: *92*; see also 26: *40–3*.]

Incidentally, the quotations reveal how radical was Moltke's vision: the war would lead to the destruction of either Prussia or Austria. Bismarck was always pursuing a more limited objective – the expulsion of Austria from the rest of Germany – which could also be presented as a German policy.

Admittedly things had changed a good deal since 1860, which would make Moltke more optimistic. The military modernisation programme had been pushed through, Austria was much weaker and

Italy could be brought into play. Yet many in the Prussian government still believed that victory would take time, and time was mainly what Napoleon needed.

The same point applies to the Italian alliance. In one sense it was a masterly Prussian success; Italy could only go to war if Prussia decided to do so, whereas Prussia was not similarly tied. But the three month duration of the alliance put pressure on Prussia; Italy by June 1866 had pretty much secured her objective whatever the result of the war.

Bismarck was well aware of how risky war was. That is why he was prepared to mobilise other weapons too, such as entering into agreement with Hungarian and Slav opponents of the Habsburg regime as well as Garibaldi. As it was, swift military victory meant that this policy was never put into practice but there is little reason to doubt that *in extremis* Bismarck would have used it, if only as one last means of keeping himself in power [24, I: *309–11*; 20: *135*].

And finally there was William. It took a great deal of Bismarck's energy to persuade the king to break at last with Austria, the old and legitimate ally both in Germany and against France. Possibly it was one reason why Bismarck avoided war in the summer of 1865. Now in 1866 Austrian threats – both using the Augustenberg candidacy and finally mobilising troops – made it possible for Bismarck to argue other precedents, such as the need to avoid another Olmütz. Once the king was persuaded that Austria sought to deprive Prussia of her rightful standing in Germany, and that Austrian mobilisation represented a serious military threat, he agreed to war. It was typical of William that he now pursued the war in a spirit of self-righteousness and the next big problem Bismarck faced was persuading him to bring the war to a rapid end before international complications could develop.

The last element in Bismarck's preparations was the bid for national leadership (see above, pp. 72–3). That did not materially affect sentiments before the war. Once the war was won, however, it soon became clear that Bismarck was prepared to move towards the liberal opposition and to carry through a national programme.

[e] The course of the war

In May 1866 the military took over. Everything depended on the outcome of the war. The other German states turned out to represent no military threat at all – Prussia swept them aside in a few days. Saxon troops fought well in Bohemia alongside the Austrian army but the Prussians had no problem marching through the medium states, including Saxony, which stood against them.

Austria was also weakened by having to divert soldiers to Italy where they fought quite effectively. The decisive confrontation was to come in Bohemia (see [26] for details of the war up to and including the battle of Königgrätz). Leaving aside the detail of the Seven Weeks War three things appear to have been decisive. First, the planning, mobilisation and concentration of the Prussian army proceeded in a new and generally effective way. The numbers involved on both sides were unprecedented. Nearly half-a-million soldiers took part directly in the battle of Königgrätz; more than at the Battle of Leipzig in 1813, greatest of all the Napoleonic battles [26: *12–13*]. The Austrians had a larger army but 100,000 of their soldiers formed the Army of the South against Italy, leaving some 175,000 Austrians and 32,000 Saxons in the Army of the North to face about 254,000 Prussian soldiers in Bohemia.

It was the Prussians who proved most effective in getting such large numbers of soldiers into action. Moltke had established special organisations to plan transportation [148: *chs 2 & 3*; 62: *39–47*]. This took advantage of the benefits conferred by the railways in bringing soldiers quickly to the mountain passes into Bohemia. Nevertheless, even Prussian troop and supply movements were delayed by many mistakes and blockages [148: *61–6*]. Moltke also decided to concentrate his troops only on the field of battle, bringing the army through the mountains in three separate groups. This conflicted with conventional military wisdom (and has been criticised subsequently) because it meant Prussian troops were widely dispersed until shortly before (or even while) battle was joined but in the event it worked.

Second, weaponry made a big difference. The needle-gun gave the Prussian infantry a huge advantage and the Austrian doctrine of 'cold steel' could not be put into practice. On the other hand, it is generally agreed that Austrian artillery outgunned the Prussians and her cavalry were more effectively used, even if both sides failed to exploit their reconnoitring role fully.

Finally, it has been argued that the Prussian officers led and the ordinary soldiers fought better than their Austrian counterparts. The evidence does not support this view. The problem was rather one of strategic leadership. Above all, the Austrians had no planning instrument to match that of the Prussian General Staff. At the highest level of all Benedek was to prove far inferior to Moltke in his grasp of the situation and ability to make the right fundamental decisions. Nevertheless, this was partly because the superior mobilisation of Prussia meant that she always held the initiative. Benedek was always on the defensive and any bold move to reverse this carried huge risks. The information available was never clear enough to justify such risks.

These matters are still debated amongst military historians. Some argue that different, and perfectly feasible, decisions by Benedek, the commander of the Austrian Army of the North, could have led to very different outcomes, especially if he had moved forward to attack one of the dispersed Prussian army groups before it could join up with the other groups. The result was, however, stunning. Within six weeks of the beginning of the war, the Austrians had been routed on the battlefields of Bohemia and were falling back to defend Vienna.

To understand this fully, however, we must step back from the war. Why was Prussia militarily so superior in 1866 and why was this so unexpected? The brief answer is that there had been a dramatic shift in the military balance of power over just a few years. The reasons for that go far beyond the confines of a narrow military history.

Austria had remained a great military power after 1815. Prussia had not. Especially after the war-scares of 1830 her army had been run down. As late as 1859 Austrian military expenditure was greater than that of Prussia. Then from 1860 Prussian expenditure sharply increased as Austria's sharply decreased. Until 1865 Prussia could only contemplate a challenge to Austria if Austria was either engaged in war with another major power (1859) or paralysed by domestic crisis (1849–50).

Prussia had demilitarised and had also developed a constitutional political system between 1830 and 1860. She had retained a short-term conscript system (the only power to do so) but this was only sustainable given that most of those liable for military service were not actually conscripted. It was feasible in Prussia to create the basis of a mass army on this short-term conscript system. First, there was internal political stability and the expansion took place during a period of rapid economic growth. Constitutional opposition was not to the fiscal or personal burdens entailed by the reforms but rather to the exclusion of parliament from the decision-making process.

The new transportation possibilities opened up by steam power meant that far larger armies than ever before could be mobilised, moved to the theatre of war and supplied. A long-term conscript, professional army could not furnish sufficient numbers to exploit this. Prussia was best placed to move in this direction before any other power. Furthermore, political stability and lack of regional tensions of the kind that beset Austria meant that serving and reserve soldiers could be based in their home territory, the best way of maintaining such forces in peacetime and yet being able to mobilise them quickly for war.

Austria's weakness was a product of power. It was financial crisis induced by military preparations and war in the 1850s which led to a reduction of military strength in the early 1860s (and which may even have weakened her economically). Prussia's lack of commitments helped economic growth and put her in a position to increase military expenditure without causing a general crisis.

Prussia could also innovate more thoroughly. A compact territory and a lack of regional diversity made central control of military affairs easier than in Austria. Ironically, the very lack of military experience made it easier to bring untried men and methods to the fore. Benedek was put in charge of the Army of the North on the strength of his battlefield record in Italy; Moltke was put in charge of the Prussian army on the strength above all of his organisational and planning skills.

Other armies had contemplated and then rejected the adoption of the breech-loading rifle. In their view the ability of soldiers to fire and reload in the prone position, and to fire more rapidly than with muzzle-loaders, would lead to a breakdown of collective discipline and the wasteful use of ammunition. Prussia had to introduce an intensive six-month training course for NCOs and junior officers in order to safeguard against this. That in turn required that soldiers at that level had the schooling necessary for them to learn effectively (e.g. by reading training manuals) and that the army command felt it could trust them. Prussia, with a short-term conscript army and the best primary education system in Europe, was uniquely placed to engage in such retraining. Later army commands, despite their generally conservative values, would press hard for better elementary education in order to introduce modernising reforms into the army.

By contrast Austria had a highly regionalised society, long-term conscripts who were difficult to retrain, an established military elite which would not easily accept the imposition of new methods of control and war, and a state treasury which could not afford to expand and innovate. She was just beginning to establish a constitutional system which could only bed itself in if over-heavy fiscal demands were avoided. Her economy might generally be growing healthily but it could not be so effectively exploited by government as it could in Prussia. The less developed capital goods industry associated with railway building and the coal, iron and steel industries meant that she lacked a railway network or a domestic military industry comparable to those of Prussia. It was possible to buy better weapons from abroad but financial crisis reduced that option.

Four conclusions can be drawn from this. First, the military balance of power had shifted very sharply from Austria to Prussia over a very few years. Second, no one, not even Bismarck or Moltke, fully realised this, let alone understood many of the conditions of such a shift. Third, the shift did not make Prussian victory inevitable; it merely made it probable whereas just five years earlier it would have been improbable. Fourth, these were not necessarily long-term trends, especially when one includes the international context. Kennedy has argued that economic strength is the key to military and political power [15]. Generally this is persuasive. However, it must be severely qualified in respect to 1866. (For a more general critique of Kennedy see Mann [14].) In general economic, let alone demographic, terms Prussia was not stronger than Austria. A short war, in any case, tests only the immediate military capacities of the states involved, not their underlying economic strengths. Weaker states can find allies to counteract their weakness. Prussian economic growth rates were exceptionally high in the 1860s and fell back later in the century. Finally, a stronger economy is often the effect rather than the cause of successful war. It is frustrating that statisticians often compare German figures to Austrian figures before 1866–71 as well as after, thereby overstating Austrian weakness. The statistics themselves assume what remained in doubt until then – namely that Prussia would bring the rest of Germany under her control. That might make sense to economic historians concerned to plot long-range change but it obscures the short-term balance of power.

Bismarck was 'lucky'. The 'great men' of history always are; their greatness lies in the fact that their particular qualities are precisely the right ones for the circumstances in which they find themselves, circumstances they neither created nor fully appreciated. So it was in 1866. However, there was no automatic route from military success to political achievement. It was in plotting this route that Bismarck's political genius was to become clear.

[f] The outcome of the war

Many historians have exaggerated the extent of Bismarck's achievements in laying the groundwork for the war against Austria. Britain and Russia were always unlikely to intervene; Italy was anxious to use the Austro-Prussian conflict to secure Venice; Bismarck's rather desperate threats to consort with Habsburg rebels never materialised; the German national movement looked on aghast and impotent; the significant German states supported Austria; French policy was only undone by the rapid, comprehensive and unexpected Prussian military success. Indeed, one could argue that any ordinary statesman in Berlin bent on war with Austria would not have done significantly worse.

The political genius in Bismarck was rather displayed during and immediately after the war.

In Prussia, on 3 July, that is the day of Königgrätz but before news of the victory, there had been elections to the *Landtag*. The results were a decisive defeat for the liberal opposition, demonstrating the importance of Prussian patriotism [17: 8–9]. The war manifesto had been couched almost entirely in terms of Prussian interests and honour [see text in 228: 66–8]. For a 'normal' conservative this situation, especially when followed by military victory, was a clear signal to settle the constitutional crisis in favour of the monarchy.

Bismarck did precisely the opposite. He introduced into the *Landtag* what is known as the Indemnity Bill. In effect Bismarck offered a settlement to the *Landtag*: a return to constitutional rule. The government would put its measures before parliament for approval in the ordinary way; parliament would not seek retribution for its treatment since 1862. Bismarck did not admit to any wrongdoing. He still adhered to the 'constitutional gap' theory on which he had justified his actions since September 1862. In principle, therefore, he could always return to that method of government if parliament and crown once more came into conflict. Nevertheless, this was a major concession to parliament and liberalism given the strong position

Bismarck now occupied. He could have just as easily modified the constitution to weaken the position of parliament. For conservatives who regarded the constitution as a gift from the crown, one that could be revoked at the king's pleasure, that is what should have been done.

Why did Bismarck behave in this way? We must remember that in many ways he was a product of modern political conditions. He was well aware of the importance of favourable public opinion, especially from those middle-class circles who dominated the press and the most dynamic parts of the growing economy. The political forces representing such groups might have suffered a temporary setback in the 1866 elections but in the longer term it was a weak government which did not command their support. Bismarck constantly talked about the need to have the support of the major social groups, although it is not always clear what he meant by this. Parliament in his view was not an instrument of government – indeed he insisted that a person could not be a deputy and a minister at the same time – but it was a vital way of consulting with and gaining the support of powerful social forces. He was also concerned that Prussia show a united face to the outside world, especially Austria and France. Later he would add the point that constitutionalism offered the best way of integrating the newly annexed territories into Prussia and of persuading the south German states that the new political creation was not authoritarian Prussia writ large [23, I: *308–14*; 226: *318–19*; 227, II: *62–4*]. The idea of appealing to German nationality in a way that went beyond cynical rhetoric and extended to alterations in the way the state was organised now became a part of Bismarck's policy.

Furthermore, Bismarck had negative memories of the conservative intrigues of the 1850s. He had no more wish to fall into the hands of the 'ultras' at court and in the army than into those of parliamentary liberals. In pushing through the Indemnity Bill Bismarck was in part preserving his independence, occupying a fulcrum position that enabled him to play off counterposing interests and institutions against one another. (This is a central argument of Gall [23, I].)

The effect of the Indemnity Bill was to divide Prussian liberals between a minority who could not put behind them four years of unconstitutional rule and harassment and a majority who saw this as a golden opportunity to help shape the new Germany that would arise out of Prussian victory. It helped Bismarck that he made this conciliatory offer from a position of strength, rather than as a concession when in an embattled position. (On liberal responses see [146: *123–9*; 17: *9–11*].)

Bismarck's other major concern was to bring the war to a rapid conclusion. William, now that he was roused to a spirit of vengeful self-righteousness, contemplated marching south and occupying Vienna, and the army leadership also wanted to consolidate their victory. Bismarck opposed this. He knew that one or two successful battles do not necessarily finish a war. To push Austria into a humiliating position would encourage a spirit of resistance in that country, the raising of new armies, the problems of occupation. In the meantime, Napoleon was starting to move to take advantage as he had always planned. Russia had hoped for Austrian success and envisaged intervening although she received no encouragement from Britain [23, I: *306–8*; 24, I: *311–16*; 13: *166–9*; 21: *238–49*].

In one sense Bismarck always held to the policy of dualism. Prussia could never conquer Austrian Germany. It was not clear how easily Prussia could gain control of south Germany, especially the Catholic states of Bavaria and Württemberg. In his memoirs Bismarck constantly stresses the way in which different areas such as Austrian Silesia or even the Protestant region of north Bavaria owed loyalty to their present ruler and that it would weaken Prussia to take over such areas. In addition Austrian Germany was a part of the Habsburg Empire, an essential element of the stability of Europe. *In extremis* Bismarck might have contemplated action which threatened to break up the empire but once the war had been resolved in Prussia's favour that was no longer necessary [226: *302–12*; 227, II: *39–54*].

Bismarck – probably helped by Napoleon's intrigues – prevailed upon William, although only after a great deal of argument which exhausted Bismarck, upset the king and offended many military men who wished to continue with the war. The peace settlement was very generous: no territory or indemnity was claimed from Austria. (Taylor [13] dissents from this view but given what Moltke and Wilhelm were contemplating it is difficult to see why.) Isolated, her major armies in disarray in the north and locked in a struggle in Italy as well, Austria was glad to accept and the Peace of Prague was soon agreed.

Prussia was less charitable to the Protestant rulers of north and central Germany who had opposed her in the war. The King of Hannover, the Elector of Hesse and the Duke of Nassau were in effect deposed and their territories annexed directly to Prussia. Bismarck calculated that it was better to destroy these dynasties completely rather than to leave them any territory and a base from which to plot recovery. He also judged that many of the subjects of these states could be reconciled to Prussian rule. Schleswig and Holstein also became a Prussian province. After a period of direct rule under military and civilian commissars these new provinces were incorporated into Prussia on the same administrative and constitutional terms as the old provinces [141].

Prussia also had to give some form to her new influence in north and central Germany. Here she put into practice elements of the plan for federal reform issued in March 1866. The states north of the river Main (including half of Hesse-Darmstadt) not annexed to Prussia joined with her in the North German Confederation. Governmental powers were vested in a *Bundesrat*, over which William presided, made up of state delegations and dominated by Prussia. The Confederation also had a lower house, a *Reichstag*, which was to be elected by all males of 25 years of age or above. In this way Bismarck hoped to convince critics in both northern and southern Germany worried about the expansion of Prussian power that the new Germany would have a genuinely popular and national character. The National Liberal party won the first elections to this *Reichstag* and cooperated closely with Bismarck for the next decade [146: *ch. 4*; 197: *104–27*].

Four considerations were to dominate German politics between 1867 and 1871. First, Prussia had to absorb and integrate her new territories and the North German Confederation had to develop a firm institutional life. Second, there was the question of relations between northern Germany and the German states south of the river Main. Third, revanchism in Austria needed to be handled. Fourth, there was the question of France, which had gained nothing from the war between Austria and Prussia. (For a general treatment of these issues see [17: *ch. 1*].)

Bismarck's own position was transformed by the success of 1866. A member of the king's entourage told Bismarck on the afternoon of 3 July, as Prussian victory became clear: 'You are now a great man. But if the crown prince had arrived too late, you would be the greatest scoundrel in the world' [Quoted in 16: *909*]. Many of Bismarck's most vociferous critics who had condemned the civil war and deplored the likelihood that it would weaken Germany as a whole as well as the two German powers, now confessed that they had been wrong and he had been right. Finally they could see a clear way forward to the forming of a German state. The cult of Bismarck, the statesman of genius who had to be uncritically followed because he saw so much further than others, began at Königgrätz.

[iii] The Franco-Prussian war

[a] Europe

So far as the major powers apart from France were concerned, nothing much changed after 1867. In August 1866 Russia had come forward with the idea of playing a mediating role in Germany but Bismarck, calling upon his populist reform plans, argued that such mediation would outrage German opinion [13: *175*; 21: *243–9*]. Russia remained estranged from Austria. The shift of political influence from the German to the Hungarian half of the Habsburg Empire, expressed in the new constitution of 1867, strengthened Habsburg determination to maintain Austria's position in south-east Europe and this was bound to cause tension with Russia. Although the new man in power, Count Beust, wished to revenge Königgrätz, this hostile relationship to Russia, amongst other factors, constrained the extent to which an anti-Prussian policy could be actively pursued [22: *85–96*].

Russian conservatives were concerned about the treatment of legitimate German princes but not enough to threaten intervention. The securing of Prussian control over Schleswig raised anxieties about Baltic–North Sea routes but Prussia did nothing to intensify such anxieties. Russia was especially anxious about the effect of a Franco-Austrian victory over Prussia. The consequence was that Russia would threaten to act in support of Prussia in 1870 in the event of Austrian mobilisation against Prussia [21: *306*].

British opinion, although regretting war as the method, was satisfied with advances made for national and liberal causes in Italy and Germany. France was still regarded as the major threat to European stability and there was a strong sense of relief that the rapid end to the war had prevented the French from interfering. British opinion also favoured Prussia against France in the political intrigues that followed concerning French 'compensation' after 1866. But even when the British government grew somewhat disenchanted with the obduracy of the Prussians as well as the ambitions of the French in the dispute over Luxemburg in 1867, public opinion was overwhelmingly in favour of a policy of non-intervention [124: *ch. 2*; 21: *ch. 9*].

Napoleon was desperate to gain something from the new situation. Opinion in France hardened against Prussia with the awareness that a major new power with territories on the left bank of the Rhine now existed [67]. Napoleon was increasingly unpopular at home and making concessions to parliamentary participation in the affairs of government [119: *187–96*]. The ambitions of obtaining Belgium or Rhineland territory had come and gone. Now, in 1867, he raised increasingly forcibly the idea of Luxemburg. This was bound in personal union with the Netherlands, whose king was willing to consider selling Luxemburg to France but only with Prussia's blessing. It was difficult for France to exert pressure on Prussia to do this short of war. Once the matter became public knowledge there was a storm of protest in Germany, making it impossible for France to pursue the matter further [13: *176–83*; 124: *chs 3–5*; 21: *262–70*; 17: *15–18*].

Napoleon now turned to strengthening his position at home with a series of liberalising measures. These made the regime even more dependent on popular opinion. In May 1870 there was a plebiscite on a new constitution. The new ministers who came to power in 1869–70 were strongly anti-Prussian. The army was being expanded and improved. By 1870 France felt herself better placed to fight Prussia than three years earlier [119: *ch. 5*; 28: *29–39*].

It would be even better if France could construct an anti-Prussian alliance. There was no prospect of help from Russia or Britain. Italy was of little use, especially as the remaining issue for Italian nationalists was Papal power in Rome which was sustained by French soldiers. So long as Catholic feeling bound Napoleon to that policy, he could not promote positive ties with Italy. In the war of 1870–1 Italy was to exploit French defeat and take control of Rome.

France's best prospect was Austria. The peace settlement in 1866 had been generous but it was still a bitter defeat. The former prime minister of Saxony, Count Beust, took over in Vienna and his central concern was to regain Austrian influence in Germany. An alliance with France directed against Prussia was the most obvious way of achieving this.

However, there was strong internal opposition to Beust's policies. The Hungarians had encouraged war in 1866 because it could provide them with an opportunity to force more concessions from Vienna. This they were able to do and the Hungarian half of the empire was granted very great autonomy in the 1867 constitution, with the Magyars confirmed in a position of dominance over the other nationalities and also with much more influence at the centre than hitherto. German influence in the western half of the empire was also weakening, especially in the face of Czech political advance. These new national groupings had no wish to see their advances put in jeopardy by a policy that could lead to renewed conflict with Prussia and which could only either weaken the empire still further or assist German Austrians to regain some of the ground they had lost in 1866. Austria's financial and military situation had worsened with the defeat of 1866 and she could not afford an expensive programme of military modernisation. All this, coupled with her turn to affairs in south-eastern Europe, meant that it was difficult for Beust to pursue an anti-Prussian policy effectively. He could encourage the French to take an anti-Prussian line but he could offer France little in return, especially if French demands were limited to Europe and could appear anti-German. Russian support of Prussia also inhibited Austrian policy [21: *esp. 283–312*; 48: *167–78*; 101; 58: *30–59*; 22: *85–97*; 142; 13: *184–97*].

By early 1870 France had secured no gains or allies against Prussia. However, she was confident that military preparations placed her in a position of advantage to Prussia and that if a war went well, then support from other quarters (Austria and also Denmark) would be forthcoming. Both her government and public opinion were very sensitive to the failures of France's German policy and were determined to suffer no further setbacks in relation to Prussia, even in matters of mere prestige. A regime which was an affront to conventional dynasties was as alive to issues of honour as any of those dynasties, transplanting that sensitivity from the honour of princes to that of nations. Ironically it would be a conventional dynastic issue, a royal succession dispute, that triggered that sense of honour and sent France to war in 1870.

France was outraged to hear that on 2 July 1870 Prince Leopold, a member of the House of Hohenzollern, had been offered the vacant throne of Spain. France regarded Spain as part of her sphere of influence. The French government refused to believe that Leopold would have allowed his name to be put forward without the knowledge and support of William, Bismarck and the Prussian government. The French demanded the withdrawal of the candidacy and an undertaking from Prussia that it would never again support such a candidacy. For two weeks France pursued this maximalist policy. Eventually she was prepared to forgo a promise from King William never again to support such a candidacy but this was a private view within the government. French policy in public appeared obdurate and, to most European opinion, unreasonable. Until the French defeats and the formation of a French republic, most European governments and their public opinions favoured Prussia. The French policy meant that Prussia could turn the Hohenzollern candidacy into a justification for war if she so wished [51; 155; 27; 20: *183–203*].

[b] Germany

In the North German Confederation the disputes with France had a marked impact on opinion. The debates over the constitution of the Confederation in 1867 had been accompanied by the diplomatic crisis over Luxemburg. This helped the cause of those who wished to stress the 'national' element in the Confederation and to come to terms with Bismarck in drawing up a practical constitution. The National Liberal movement was strong not just in 'old' Prussia but also in 'new' Prussia, that is the newly annexed territories. For many Germans living in these territories incorporation into Prussia and the North German Confederation provided opportunities to play a much more effective political role than had been possible before. Bourgeois national and liberal sentiments had been stifled under the estates-government of the Duchies of Schleswig and Holstein as well as under the military occupations of Austria and Prussia. The same was true for political life in the arbitrary and outmoded princely regimes of Hannover, Electoral Hesse and Nassau. It is no accident that the two most important figures of the National Liberal Party in the early Second Empire – Rudolf Bennigsen and Johannes Miquel – were Hannoverians. They could point to a more efficient and cheaper administration, liberal reforms and constitutional government, as well as positive involvement in a great national cause, as the benefits to be had from Prussian victory. Furthermore, these liberals had no bitter memories of conflict with Bismarck during the constitutional crisis of 1862–6 [146: *123–40*; 141 on the annexations process; 161 for a regional study].

Prussia strengthened her national and liberal credentials in northern and central Germany by building on the strong Protestant-flavoured national culture that had been constructed before 1867 and carrying through a range of unifying yet liberalising social and economic measures [17: *7–22*; 19: *chs 7 & 8*]. On other matters such as control of the military budget liberals were unable to make progress. (For the involvement of particular liberals see the English-language biographies of Eduard Lasker [90] and Ludwig Bamberger [166].)

There were strong critics of the new politics. Catholics both in 'old' Prussia and 'new' Prussia felt they had suddenly become an endangered species with the removal of Austrian protection and the fellowship of south German Catholics in the old Confederation. Tension was heightened as the Pope condemned liberalism in his Syllabus of Errors (1864) and declared the doctrine of Papal infallibility (1870). This was accompanied by a Catholic revivalism. National liberals were very hostile to these developments which they considered reactionary and anti-national. The conflict pushed Bismarck and national liberals closer together and stimulated the growth of a popular and oppositional political Catholicism [151; 45: *85–95*; 163; 146: *135–7*].

There were also left-liberal and radical critics who opposed the 1867 settlement as greater Prussian authoritarian rule with just a few insignificant concessions to liberal and popular demands [150: *168–71*; 78: *70–123*]. Finally, many conservatives, in Prussia as well as in other states, were unhappy with the innovative features of the new politics such as the destruction of legitimate dynasties, the appeal to national feeling and a parliament based on the masses [23, I: *311–12*; 209: *Pt II*].

However, these political opponents were divided and in disarray. Given favourable economic conditions and the many liberalising measures carried through under National Liberal initiatives in the Prussian and North German parliaments, the new national politics could be regarded as a great success.

This was not the case in the south German states, especially Württemberg and Bavaria. Prussian power had stopped short of the Main but it still looked very threatening. Bismarck had persuaded William out of annexations and territorial reorganisation south of the Main but Prussia undoubtedly had the military strength to carry through such a policy, at least in the short term. As it was the southern states were compelled to enter into a secret defensive and offensive military agreement with Prussia. This tied them to Prussian diplomacy in a very dangerous manner. In 1867, in the midst of the Luxemburg crisis, Bismarck ensured that these alliances became public knowledge. If the intention was to strengthen national feeling in south Germany it failed. Many south Germans were upset to find how closely their governments had tied them to Prussian policies which might after all lead to war with Catholic powers such as France or Austria. The attempts to harmonise south German military institutions with those of Prussia proved highly unpopular. To come into line with Prussia it would be necessary to introduce conscription into south Germany and to increase military expenditure. For states with a strong tradition of low military expenditure and suspicion of over-powerful standing armies these were unwelcome measures. By 1870 the attempts by the Bavarian and Württemberg governments to implement these military policies had led to crises in both states [20: *161–78*].

North and south German states were economically linked through the Zollverein. In 1867 Prussia came forward with the idea of having a Customs Union parliament. In this parliament members of the North German Reichstag would be joined by deputies from south Germany elected by universal manhood suffrage. This *Zollparlament* would not have many powers but it was considered one way in which it would be possible to appeal to 'national' feeling over the heads of south German governments. Elections were held in early 1868. The plan backfired. National liberals in each of the states had expected to do well. However, especially in Württemberg and Bavaria, anti-Prussian political groups – an unlikely alliance of particularists, political Catholics and democrats – secured a majority of seats [17: *19*]. There continued to be powerful national liberal elements in each of the states including the Baden government. Figures in the Bavarian government such as Hohenloe argued that it would be better to negotiate entry into a new all-German political system from a position of strength rather than leaving it to a time when Prussia could dictate the terms. However, these various liberals and pragmatists, especially in Bavaria and Württemberg, were outnumbered and defeated by anti-Prussian sentiment. In certain respects Germany looked further away from unity in May 1870 than she had done in 1867.

[c] Prussia

After 1867 Bismarck's major concern was to absorb what Prussia had gained in northern and central Germany. At the same time he sought to build bridges with the south German states by various peaceful means. The two policies conditioned one another. Bismarck was constrained in how he behaved in north Germany by his awareness of its likely impact on opinion in south Germany. Internationally his main concern was to ward off any interference with his German programme. That could include, as in the case of the Luxembourg crisis, appeals to national sentiment. One consequence of such appeals was to popularise anti-French sentiments amongst Germans, especially but not exclusively in northern and Protestant parts of Germany. Inexorably Bismarck was having to stress the national character of Prussian and North German policy [24, I: *chs 16–18*; 23, I: *314–44*].

However, this could not be pushed ahead too quickly. Any idea that the government was aggressively pursuing a national path could alarm the international community as well as the south German states. This was why Bismarck quashed the National Liberal idea of inviting Baden to join the North German Confederation. The Baden government was willing to do this but Bismarck feared the impact on the other south German states as well as international feeling. He would sooner that Baden continued as a pro-Prussian element in southern Germany than that she was detached from the rest of the south [20: *175–6*; 24, I: *430–1*].

These cautious forward policies were faltering by early 1870. In northern Germany Bismarck was more dependent on the National Liberals than he liked. In south Germany his military and customs union policies had proved counterproductive. Rather desperate ideas such as restoring the imperial title in early 1870 failed, partly due to the rejection by the kings of Bavaria and Württemburg [24, I: *431–4*]. At the same time the danger existed that the governments of Bavaria and Württemberg might fall because of their pro-Prussian policies in the matter of military reform. Then Bismarck would have faced a serious problem as to whether to interfere in their defence. That could both have created international complications and increased anti-Prussian sentiments in southern Germany. There were also some grounds for concern at the policies of Beust. In both cases the real cause for concern was the opportunities this would present France to weaken Prussia's position in Germany [20: *174–6*; 65: *92–6*; 13: *192–7*; 24, I: *434–59*].

The significance of the Hohenzollern candidacy has to be seen against this background. Both then and later Bismarck denied having knowledge of the candidacy until shortly before it became public. For a long time documents, especially from the Hohenzollern-Sigmarinen archive, were kept secret from historians who might have used them in ways which could discredit German foreign policy. Since World War II, however, it has been established that Bismarck knew about the issue as soon as it had arisen with approaches from Madrid to Leopold's father, Prince Anton. Anton had turned to King William, as Head of the House of Hohenzollern, for guidance. Bismarck advised William to support the candidacy. Without that support Leopold would not have allowed his name to go forward [155; 51; 27; 21: *183–203*].

One can speculate as to Bismarck's motives. That he was planning to use the candidacy to bring about war with France is implausible. In his unreliable memoirs Bismarck has to balance his claim to have known war was inevitable and to be planning for it with his protestations of innocence in the matter of the Hohenzollern candidacy. Nevertheless, he makes the important point that it was irrational for the French to believe that a Hohenzollern on the Spanish throne could really have altered diplomatic relations. Given that, it was impossible to predict that the French would prove as intransigent as they did. After all, the French did gain the withdrawal of the candidacy and effectively of Prussian support for such a candidacy in future. (William had always had his doubts about the value of a Hohenzollern taking so insecure a throne.) France could now have turned her attention to gaining a positive outcome in Madrid. (For Bismarck's claim to regard war with France as inevitable if the unification of Germany was to be completed see [226: *314–15*]; for the Hohenzollern candidacy [226: *334–7*; 227, II: *58, 87–91*].)

It seems more likely that for Bismarck this was a case of having one more iron in the fire which might provide some diplomatic gains in Spain; which could be used as a means of influencing relations with France; and which could always be dropped without too much difficulty if that should seem expedient [23, I: *348–9*; 24, I: *459–62*; 20: *183–203*].

By July 1870, however, Bismarck had decided upon war. At the famous meeting between Benedetti, the French ambassador, and

William in Bad Ems, William withdrew his support for the candidacy and went on to venture the hope that this could lead to the restoration of friendly relations between France and Prussia. The French government had privately agreed that this would be enough to defuse the situation, even if they had instructed Benedetti to demand an undertaking that Prussia would never again support such a candidacy. Bismarck doctored the wording of the telegram from William to Berlin reporting on the interview with Benedetti so that this maximalist demand and William's rejection of it as improper was given prominence, drawing attention away from the effective Prussian climbdown and the sense that negotiations could continue. The French government now felt that it had no option but to pursue the matter further, leading to war [228: *92–5*; 2: *225–9*].

In July 1870 Bismarck deliberately spurned the opportunity to avoid war, even if it was the French who actually pushed the decision on to war itself. Three reasons can be offered for this decision. First, there remained fears that Beust in Vienna might eventually bring Austria around to an anti-Prussian alliance. To destroy the French threat now would permanently remove that possibility. Second, there was the problem that the south German states were slipping away. A national war against the old enemy in which the French appeared the aggressors, a war to which the terms of the military alliance bound the southern states, would reverse that slippage. Finally, and perhaps most important, was the judgement that the French would continue to press upon Prussia to make concessions and accept, as with Italy, some kind of client status. A liberalised French government, mobilising rather than resisting its own popular opinion and continuing with military improvements, might well turn out to be a more formidable opponent in a few more years. Such were the grounds for Moltke's view that war should be fought sooner rather than later. He had long taken this view [28: *41–2*]. (For the most recent German-language assessments of the origins of the war of 1870–1 see [194 & 195].)

[d] The war and its outcome

Both sides were confident of victory. On this occasion Prussia did not have clear superiority in the weapons of her infantry. The French *chassepot* was to prove at least as effective as the needle-gun. Prussia had, however, improved her artillery since 1866 [148: *Pt III, esp.*

216–21; 28: *ch. 1*]. Perhaps the main reason for the Prussian victory, however, was the speed of her mobilisation and the concentration of troops against the enemy so that she fought and defeated two separate French armies. At the same time, as is usually the case in wars, the losing side made the most mistakes. As with the Austrians in 1866 the French appeared paralysed by the speed of the German advance and were in a constant state of both strategic and tactical indecision. Strategically they could not decide between advancing, holding border areas and fortresses, or withdrawing, even as far as taking up a defensive position around Paris. Tactically they failed – as Benedek had failed in 1866 – to move out of defensive positions such as Metz and attack German armies when these were dangerously divided and weak. The net result was that one army was bottled up in Metz and the other dithered between forward and backward movement and was destroyed and captured at Sedan [28].

The numbers mobilised exceeded by far those of the war of 1866. Within eighteen days of beginning mobilisation well over one million soldiers had reported for duty in Germany and nearly half-a-million were transported to the French frontier. By the end of the war Germany had over 800,000 men under arms. The French took longer to move; by the end of July they had fewer than 250,000 mobilised in the Army on the Rhine. Numbers continued to expand but not quickly enough and the Army of Chalon, the second French army, was heavily outnumbered at Sedan. After the crucial defeats in August and at Sedan on 1 September, the new French republic did mobilise over half-a-million soldiers. The main problem was that the early losses – dead, wounded and captured – deprived these soldiers of experienced leadership. But altogether over one-and-a half million men were enrolled in the opposing armies. Nothing like this had ever been seen before in Europe. (The American Civil War in which the Union side deployed modern industrial capacity and the Confederate side dipped deep into its (white) manpower provided a precedent but had been largely ignored in Europe.)

Unlike the war of 1866 this was a national war, arguably the first of its kind [17: *27–30*]. (The most recent study of French and German attitudes towards one another in 1870 is Jeismann [192].) The German national movement engaged fully behind the Prussian government. The princes of southern Germany brought their states into the war and south German troops fought as effectively as their counterparts from the north. One must not exaggerate this and certainly it would be wrong to explain it in terms of deep-rooted national antagonisms. As recently as 1813 the south German states – Napoleonic creations – had been allies with Catholic France against Protestant Prussia. French attitudes towards Germany until 1870 had never been as negative and hostile as towards either Britain or Russia. In part the war produced the sentiments that are sometimes supposed to have brought it about. French patriotism was engaged by military defeat; German patriotism by military success. That in turn led on to a more bitter war, especially on the French side.

This national war roused demands for a much more comprehensive victory than in 1866. Bismarck did not seek to bring about peace after the initial victorious battles and the fall of Napoleon, not because of national pressure but rather because he saw the situation as a very different one from that of 1866. Early successes served to ensure France's isolation and to remove any fear of intervention by other powers. National emotions had to be satisfied. Bismarck regarded France as unpredictable, lacking a stable and legitimate government with which one could come to binding agreements [28: *218–25*]. Nevertheless, Bismarck did not go as far as those like Moltke who would have favoured a war of much more extreme destruction.

For the time being Bismarck, Moltke and national opinion were at one and the war was carried forward to a siege of Paris and an occupation of much of France. The new republican government raised fresh armies and mobilised popular patriotism against the German invaders. Its own efforts were divided with the Paris Commune which, although itself patriotic and anti-German, represented a threat to the republican government itself. The Prussian army stood aside to watch a veritable civil war as the Commune was bloodily repressed by the French government. This internal political division also helps to explain France's defeat. Whereas Prussia built her military reforms on the basis of universal conscription, unworried about the political loyalties of her soldiers and able to override liberal objections, the more bourgeois society of France, with its fear of popular radicalism, had rejected such a military system when it was proposed in the 1860s. The French needed to be defeated before they would rally under arms. By then, however, under the new conditions of warfare, it was too late. There was to be no Valmy *à la*

1792; no successful *levée en masse*; no Napoleon Bonaparte [28; 119: *197–205*].

Bismarck had not resisted the radicalising effects of sustained war. Nor did he prove moderate in bringing the war to an end. The peace settlement was vengeful. Alsace and Lorraine were annexed to Germany. Partly this was justified on the grounds of strategic security. Partly nationalist arguments were employed. Heinrich von Treitschke, for example, declared that the inhabitants of Alsace were German. If they had 'forgotten' this, they must be brought back to their 'true' nationality even against their own conscious will. A new kind of nationalism, stressing language and even race, was being born, threatening to displace a view of nationality which stressed choice and participation [17: *29–32*; 31: *125–8*; 192: *241–95*].

A heavy indemnity was imposed upon France. Bismarck had no intention of upholding 'legitimate' government in France or establishing diplomatic ties with her. He assumed that France could never accept a powerful German neighbour and that policy towards France must always be solely a matter of superior strength. Of course, such a policy produced the very sentiments it claimed it was intended to contain [23, I: *361–8*; 24, I: *474–89*; 13: *212–19*].

Once victory was secured Prussia began negotiating the terms under which the south German states would enter a German state. Bismarck was sensitive to south German needs. There was no question of Prussia annexing further territory provided reasonable agreements could be made. The rulers of the south German states and the terms on which they ruled would be respected. Before a constitution was drawn up for the new state, separate treaties were negotiated with each of the states. In particular Bismarck was concerned to secure Bavarian acquiescence to the new empire and to that end included massive bribery of King Ludwig amongst his political methods. At the same time the Bavarians received special concessions such as the autonomy of their army [24, I: *490–506*].

These treaties were the most important condition of the constitution of the new empire. The preamble to that constitution presented it as the outcome of agreements between the individual states [32: *121*]. A constituent assembly played much more the role of a rubber stamp in 1870–1 than it had in 1867. Parliamentary and liberal opinion was disregarded on many issues. For example, the decision to use the term 'empire' in the title of the new polity was something with which liberals were unhappy. Bismarck could now balance the national liberal dominance in northern Germany against particularist and Catholic sentiments in southern Germany. In many respects the state of 1871 represented a turning back from the unitary, parliamentary and liberal trends displayed in the years of the North German Confederation. Parliamentary deputies were not invited to the grand ceremony to proclaim the Empire. The trappings of dynasty, court and army dominated the occasion. The 'German nation' was addressed and the empire proclaimed in its name but national institutions and language were conspicuous by their absence [54; 31: *127–9*].

On 18 January 1871 the German Empire was proclaimed in Versailles. We have numerous heroic pictures of the occasion. The most famous one is 'The Proclamation of the Emperor at Versailles' by Anton von Werner which was presented to the new German imperial art gallery in 1877. It is in the approved imperial style – realistic in detail, epic in conception. Yet in certain respects it tells a misleading story. One trivial point is that Bismarck is portrayed in a white uniform, not the colour he actually wore. Less trivially, this change was made the better to stress the centrality of Bismarck. Actually the ceremony proved trying for Bismarck and he did not dominate it, by all accounts reading out a statement 'To the German Nation' rapidly and in an ill-temper. There had been arguments about the precise terms under which William would be declared Emperor. William favoured the title 'Emperor of Germany', the Crown Prince that of 'Emperor of the Germans'. Bismarck opposed these terms because of the offence they could cause the south Germans, appearing as a claim asserted over them. He favoured the less assertive term 'German Emperor'. In the event the Grand Duke of Baden, on whom fell the honour of raising the *vivat*, solved the problem with the meaningless phrase 'Long live the Emperor William'. William, furious, left the hall without acknowledging Bismarck's presence. This incident, trivial in itself, points to a lack of consensus, even at the very top of the German political system, about what had been created. The painting suggests that the construction of myths of consensus accompanied the institutional formation of the new nation-state from its outset [20: *207–8*; 2: *28–9* (extract from diary of Crown Prince); 24, I: *504–6*; 23, I: *372–4*].

4 Results

[i] Introduction

The result of the changes I have described in this book is usually called the unification of Germany. I have chosen to call it the formation of a German nation-state. There are certain difficulties with the term 'unification of Germany'.

If we accept at minimum the definition of Germany before 1871 as comprising the territory of the German Confederation, then the Germany that was actually created was very different. It excluded the Austrian portions of the Confederation, while including Schleswig and Alsace-Lorraine which had not been part of the Confederation.

The Crown Prince preferred to see William called Emperor of the Germans rather than of Germany. Was it Germans who were unified rather than Germany? The Imperial Constitution of 1849 declared that a German was a citizen of the German state. Nationality is treated as a function, not the basis, of citizenship. In the constitution of 1871 there is no definition of citizenship nor any account of what rights Germans as citizens would enjoy in the new *Reich* [32: *77–117, 121–45* for English translations of the two constitutions]. So we cannot get very far in fleshing out the idea of being German in this direction, unless we simply assert that Germans are the subjects of the various states that make up the new *Reich*. In legal terms that is rather unsatisfactory, especially as the legal basis of state membership varied from one state to another and had not yet been clearly supplanted by a uniform *Reich*-level definition [61: *esp. 50–72*].

If we take the view that nationality *precedes and is independent of* state membership, then the only workable definition we have of German nationality is that it comprises all those people whose first language is German. No one in mid-nineteenth-century Europe, in-

100

cluding Germans, seriously proposed any alternative non-political conception of nationality, even if such ideas, e.g. racial ones, were hinted at in some of the ways in which territorial claims were justified in 1871. If we took this definition without any qualification, then the German state of 1871 subjected Danish, Polish, and French nationals to alien rule and excluded Germans in Austria as well as many other parts of central Europe. (I leave aside the problem of where the German language ceases to be the German language, e.g. whether the Alsatian dialect as first language suffices to define inhabitants of Alsace as Germans, although this is really a political rather than a linguistic matter.)

However, this would be an impractical and anachronistic measure to take. It is impractical because in any period to base state territory simply on language or some other cultural criterion does not work since people do not distribute themselves territorially in that neat fashion. Nation-states are at best imperfect in this cultural sense and can only function in a reasonable way if people find ways of living with such imperfections. It is anachronistic because in mid-nineteenth-century Europe qualifications were added to the language criterion of nationality before it was put to political use. National liberals, in Germany and elsewhere, laid great stress upon the dominant language of an area, by which they usually meant the language of government and church officials. Closely linked to this were the historical-political affiliations of an area. It was on this basis that Danish speakers in Schleswig, Czech speakers in Austria and Polish speakers in West Prussia could be regarded as belonging to Germany, even as being politically German. We might be inclined to regard this as self-serving but it is worth noting that a similar view of the matter was taken by liberals outside Germany, just as German liberals applied the same principles to the Hungarian half of the Habsburg Empire [57: *chs 4 & 5*; 94: *ch. 1*]. Such principles underlaid the way in which liberals and radicals envisaged the redrawing of the political map of Europe in 1848–9. (See, for example, the view of Marx, who in this sense was a typical radical of his time [73: *28–48*].)

To argue that nationality should play a part in the political affairs of a state was not necessarily to argue that there should be nation-states. Many Austrian Germans were convinced that German nationality was a vital element in the states of the German Confederation but they did not wish to create a German nation-state. Indeed, shared nationality could be a vital element in ensuring good relations between states. Bismarck was clear that it was this as well as dynastic connections which would sustain good relations between a Prusso-German state and Austria. The same reasoning led Bismarck to regard the German speakers of Baltic Russia as politically Russian but as a vital ingredient, by virtue of their influence in the Csarist state, in maintaining good relations with Russia [200]. If we think of Germans as speakers of the German language, then no one wanted to unify Germans in 1870–1 – not even the most committed of German nationalists. It is important to state this clearly because there is still a widespread assumption that romantic, ethnic and even racial conceptions of nationality which envisaged gathering all Germans together in a great nation-state played a part in creating and justifying the *Reich* of 1871 [106; 128; 85]. Leaving aside the question of what role German nationalism did play in the formation of the *Reich*, such ideas were not what animated the German nationalists of the time [54].

This brings us back to the German Confederation. To define Germany as the territory of the Confederation was the only practicable or acceptable option up to 1866. Contemporaries distinguished between national territory and cultural nationality. German nationality should prevail in the German states but these states could include non-German speakers and German speakers could play an honourable part in states in which other nationalities were dominant, such as Russia.

The 'unification of Germany', however, entailed the destruction of the Confederation. 'Unification' refers not to what happened to Germans or to Germany but to the *German states*. It means the destruction of multiple sovereignties, or more precisely the transference of state sovereignty from the medium and smaller German states to Berlin where it was merged with the sovereignty of the Prussian state.

Unless and until the Habsburg Empire was destroyed, that could only happen by excluding Austria from Germany. Austrian Germany could only have formed part of a *German* state through its separation from the rest of the Habsburg Empire and the Habsburg Empire could not have survived that separation. Whether it would have been possible to relocate sovereignty under those conditions from Vienna to Berlin, as it was relocated from Munich, Stuttgart, Dresden, etc. is another matter. The main point, however, is that in the first place the stress should be on the term *state* when we consider the events of 1866–71 as leading to the formation of a *nation-state*.

That is not to argue that a Prussian-dominated German state was inevitable. One can easily imagine other possibilities. The dualist system of Austro-Prussian hegemony within the German Confederation might have continued. Austria might have prevailed over Prussia before or in 1866. She might then have reinforced the system of indirect domination through confederal arrangements (especially if Prussia had been weakened and some of the medium states strengthened) or formed a huge multinational central European state. Neither of those outcomes, however, could be described in terms of *a German nation-state* because they would either have continued a system of multiple sovereignty in Germany or concentrated sovereignty into a multinational state.

However, what this does mean is that the only *thinkable* German nation-state, that is a single sovereign and territorial state in which German nationality dominated, was a Prusso-German state. (I leave aside as highly improbable the democratic-revolutionary scenario in which the authority of the Prussian as well as other German states was destroyed from below and this in turn led to the formation of a single German state.) Only by means of Prussian state power could the Austrian state be expelled from its indirect control over other German states and those other German states compelled to surrender some of their authority to a new state.

Therefore the question to ask is not: why was the German nation-state a Prusso-German state? That was the only kind of a nation-state the German state could have been. Rather there are three more pertinent questions to ask. First, was there a German question in the first place which called for some major political transformation? Second, if there was such a question why was it resolved through the formation of a nation-state rather than by some other means? Third, what kind of a nation-state was it that was formed as a consequence?

[ii] Why the nation-state?

The historian can no more prove that what happened was inevitable than that it was accidental. History is not an experimental science in which historians can test for significance by varying the conditions and seeing what difference this makes to outcomes. We have only one outcome – the actual outcome – on which to base our accounts and interpretations. Yet in trying to understand the past historians are compelled to reason about significance and probability. How else does one decide that some actions count for more than other actions? That implies views about what might have been. It is best to make this explicit and to do this requires some disciplined 'thought-experiments'.

One can begin these by noting a series of weaknesses in the political arrangements of the German Confederation, in order to answer the first question I have posed. Here, in the centre of Europe, were a number of small and medium states which lacked the power to sustain themselves. Weak states inevitably fall under the influence of powerful states unless they are able to play off powerful states against one another. Belgium owed her existence to British power; the Italian states before 1859 to Austrian power. The medium German states maintained semi-independence through the operation of Austro-Prussian dualism.

This dualism was becoming more and more difficult to sustain, especially after 1848. It was based upon Austrian predominance, secured in Vienna in 1814–15 and apparently reasserted at Olmütz in 1850. However, that predominance was bound to be questioned given the way in which Prussian demographic growth and economic development outstripped that of Austria. In 1815 there was rough equality in population and economic terms between the Prussian and Austrian territories of the Confederation. By 1866 there was a marked imbalance (see Tables I and II). Austrian political predominance sat uneasily with Prussian economic predominance, as is apparent when comparing the Federal Diet and the *Zollverein*.

More fundamentally, the *form* of this dualism was difficult to sustain. It was based upon the increasingly archaic idea of a union of princes who could agree to cooperate in some matters while leaving each other free to rule their individual territories. However, the development of territorially integrated states in which princes ruled through modern bureaucracies and were increasingly answerable to their subjects through constitutional rules and increasingly powerful public opinions undermined such arrangements. Princes, for example, could discuss changing the nature of the *Zollverein* but their parliaments and public opinions would not let them. The dynasties of the smaller and medium states retained an illusion of control only by conceding to such opinion while at the same time tacking between Austria and Prussia. At the same time, urbanisation and industrialisation transformed the basis of state power.

The breakdown of the old diplomatic understandings at the time of the Crimean war forced the major powers into reform programmes, military above all but also political and bureaucratic, which began to realise politically this new potential. The key to this power was not merely technological but human; the capacity to train hundreds of thousands of men to use new forms of fire-power and then to bring those men rapidly to the chosen theatre of war. Furthermore, to pay for this capacity required obtaining widespread political consent; to sustain it, new and higher levels of per capita production. Only the larger, modernising territorial states could take part in this competition and even they had to alter their political nature and broaden their basis of support. The medium and smaller states of the German Confederation were doubly hit: they represented a zone of political-military weakness which could not take part in this competition and they were a target for larger states that did engage in that competition.

For these reasons the political thinking of Schwarzenberg and Bismarck was more appropriate to the modern conditions of politics after 1850 than that of Metternich. Both Bismarck and Schwarzenberg took the view that the existing form of dualism could not function because that assumed that power could be shared on a territorial basis between states rather than recognising that the modern state was a sharply defined territorial unity in which sovereignty was asserted by specialised political institutions. Austria must prevail over Prussia or Prussia over Austria or they must create two sharply divided zones of power [33].

However, there was a vital difference. The Austrian vision of such preponderance necessarily took an imperial form: the 70-million strong state; the central European state. The Prussian vision took a national form because it was confined to and focused upon German territories. The Bismarckian vision was national in the way that the Schwarzenberg vision could not be. At the same time the Bismarckian vision was to create two territorial spheres of influence whereas the Schwarzenberg vision was to create just one. Bismarck did not aim to destroy Austrian sovereignty, merely to exclude its operation over the other German states. Schwarzenberg's vision necessarily involved the destruction of Prussian sovereignty.

One can reason that the central European ideal was impracticable. It would have called forth a union of all the other major powers against it. In any case, the Habsburg Empire lacked the strength or unity of purpose to pursue so radical a goal. In reality the policy served as a weapon against Prussia and a means of pushing politics back towards the old dualist form. Bismarck's policy was both modern and practical in that it was limited to Germany.

Under modern political conditions there are powerful pressures pushing states towards some kind of identification with their subjects. This is linked to the greater participation of people in affairs of government; with the transformation of subjects into citizens. It becomes necessary for states to claim that they act for 'their' citizens. In part this is achieved through purely political means such as constitutionalism. The individual German states sought to create citizen loyalty in this way. However, it went further than this. Individual German states promoted a sense of a common culture based on nationality, although they did not think that this carried with it the implication of a single German state. At the same time, the incomplete sovereignty of the smaller and medium states pushed political opposition up towards a national level. In addition, the increase in economic and cultural contacts across state boundaries helped to generate a range of associations and movements which defined themselves as German. In these definitions we have seen that the dominant tone was set by a kind of secular and Protestant, bourgeois and liberal ethos. It was precisely the people involved in these movements who also played the leading role in the modern sectors of economic, cultural and political life.

This reasoning suggests that, in the long term, there was a great pressure towards the elimination of the sovereign powers of the smaller and medium German states; that the national idea could play a major part in making the resultant state work effectively under modern conditions; and that Prussia was best placed to bring this about by excluding Austria from the rest of Germany.

However, to that argument one must add several large qualifications. The balance of power in Germany has historically been an integral part of the balance of power in Europe. Major political change in Germany normally only accompanies major political change more generally in Europe. However, usually when that balance of power has broken down, Germany has been as likely to fall prey to states outside as inside Germany. After the Crimean war the balance of power in Europe broke down but without being linked to a major threat to Germany from outside. The collapse of the existing alliances, especially that between Austria and Russia, created a unique set of conditions for a settlement of the German question that could be partially detached from the broader European context. This contrasts markedly with other periods of political-military transformation in the German lands which were accompanied by more general warfare and political change: the Thirty Years War, the War of Austrian Succession, the Seven Years War, the revolutionary and Napoleonic wars, and the two world wars. (Only in 1989–90 did it again prove possible to detach change in Germany – namely the takeover of the German Democratic Republic by the Federal German Republic – from the larger changes in Europe which had made that takeover possible.)

Although there were economic and cultural conditions which could make Prussian domination of non-Austrian Germany sustainable, ultimately Prussian policy was a matter of Prussian state interest and its success depended upon military victory. To try to see the importance of this distinction between underlying conditions and politico-military achievement one could ask the question: what would have happened if Prussia had lost in 1866 or in 1870–1?

If the vague Austrian war aims and last-minute agreements with France are anything to go by in 1866, the result of Prussian defeat would have been the loss of the Rhinelands and Silesia and the strengthening of the medium states at the expense of the smaller ones. Austria could not have envisaged taking more than Silesia for herself and Napoleon considered that it would be difficult actually to take over the Rhinelands rather than create a client state. Once again we see that under the conditions of modern politics there are limits, partly set by a sense of nationality, to how far populations in modern Europe can be arbitrarily transferred from one state to another. (See the case studies of such transfers in [86] under premodern conditions.) The purpose of strengthening the medium states was that only in this way could a balance be created against a still-powerful Prussia in Germany without offending national sentiment. In other words, what was envisaged was a reconstruction of a viable balance of power in Germany. Some of the leading Habsburg politicians in 1866 such as Esterhazy believed that the war would only lead to adjustments in the dualist balance of this kind [4: 99–100].

Politically this appeared plausible. Whether the Rhenish and Silesian populations would have accepted it, especially if cut off from economic relations with the rest of Prussia, is another matter. It is difficult to see that the existing customs union arrangements could have been radically altered. This suggests that there were thinkable alternatives but they would have retained much of the existing German political and economic arrangements. To have gone further would have entailed pursuing quite radical policies of occupation and control, such as were to be realised during and after war in twentieth-century Europe. That was beyond both the imagination and the capacity of any state in nineteenth-century Europe. One has only to look at the problems the *Reich* itself encountered in Alsace-Lorraine, Schleswig and Polish Prussia to see that there were strict limits on such population and territorial transfers under nineteenth-century conditions.

If France had prevailed in 1870–1 again it is difficult to imagine that she could have destroyed the North German Confederation. At most it would have been weakened through French acquisitions or the establishment of a client state in the Rhinelands and a strengthening of the autonomy of the south German states. One can hardly envisage a Napoleon restoring the deposed and largely unloved princes of northern Germany. The thinkable alternatives were even more limited in 1870–1 than they were in 1866.

One reason for these limits was the operation of international politics: the other powers would not have tolerated too great an expansion of French power in the wake of military victory in 1870. Another reason is the intangible element of nationality in the politics of the time. There was a German *Bund*, a German *Zollverein*, a German national movement.

These institutions and movements did not in any direct way wield power; ultimately that was wielded by governments, most of them dynasties, and these dynasties did not see themselves principally in nationality terms. However, they had to take account of the loyalties of actual or potential subjects. They *could* choose to acquire territories in which such loyalties did not exist but that would condition the nature of rule. Lorraine and Polish Prussia had to be governed in a different way from Hannover or Saxony.

The existence of strong national sentiments placed a check upon the prospects of 'alien' government. It also represented an asset for a 'national' government. Much more in the way of a national culture and movement had developed in the German lands than in the Italian lands by 1870. As a consequence southern Germany could be governed far more consensually from Berlin than southern Italy could be governed from Rome, even if political Catholicism did pose a problem for the German government [74]. One of Bismarck's great qualities in seeking to extend Prussian control over other German states had been his sensitivity to relating forms of rule to the loyalties of subjects, although he was more adept at the constitutional than the ideological aspect of this task.

Constructing such a cultural consensus between government and its subjects was not a purely German problem. The Habsburg state increasingly confronted such problems in the last 50 years of its life. In a different way the same attention to the needs and loyalties of subjects also had to be observed in the old nation-states of Britain and France both through changes in the political organisation of the state (extension of the franchise, adoption of new forms of government) and through an increasing emphasis upon the 'national' character of state institutions [95; 160].

I will consider the specific role of nationalism as a political movement in the formation of the German state in the next section. So far as the more general role of nationality is concerned, perhaps we should think of it as a ratchet on a wheel. It does not push the wheel forward but it prevents the wheel slipping back. The strong development of German institutions and movements under modern conditions did not directly prescribe the formation of a German nation-state. It did, however, preclude the destruction of a German political, economic and cultural zone. Within that zone, the only form a German nation-state could take was that of the Prusso-German state.

[iii] What kind of a nation-state?

A dynasty made the first German state but had to take account of the principle of nationality in doing so. There was as a consequence a difficult and ambiguous relationship between the dynastic and the national principle in the first German nation-state.

There were, to begin with, limits to the extent to which the Prussian state could have abandoned its dynastic traditions and still have created the basis of a national state. The bourgeois and popular politics of France in the 1860s unfitted her for the military challenge which was involved in any transformation of the politics of the German lands. It was an army constructed against the wishes of the German

109

national and liberal movement, both inside and beyond Prussia, which met that challenge. The army was thoroughly modern but its leadership was also thoroughly Prussian and illiberal. Yet, as we have seen, the cultural and economic conditions which laid the basis for the assertion of Prussian power in Germany represented a different kind of modernity, one in which national and liberal sentiments were of central importance. Could these different kinds of modernity which came into conflict in Prussia between 1862 and 1866 be combined?

Between 1867 and 1870 a great deal of unifying legislation had been carried through in the North German Confederation under the initiative of the National Liberals. Bismarck accepted this initiative in such areas as banking, currency, trade law and civil rights such as those of movement and settlement. Furthermore, with Prussia occupying some 90 per cent of the territory and population of the Confederation, the weight of common Prussian measures and practices had a strong unifying effect. The national liberal vision was of a modern, secular society and state developing in the area of the Confederation, undermining the outmoded powers of dynasty, aristocracy and religion. At the same time the benefits of these arrangements would make themselves increasingly clear to Germans south of the river Main who would inexorably be pulled into this modern Germany.

The national liberals and many historians have perhaps exaggerated the speed of the changes that were supposed to produce this effect. Agriculture remained the dominant economic sector until well after 1871; in certain respects, especially in Catholic areas, religious belief seems to have grown stronger rather than weaker; at least some German dynasties continued to command a good deal of power, respect and loyalty; and some aristocrats proved stubbornly capable of defending their interests. In strictly political terms the national movement played a limited role in bringing about transformation in Germany. It was ignored by both Prussia and Austria in the Schleswig-Holstein affair and the war with Denmark and again in the events leading to the Austro-Prussian war. Only following that victory did Bismarck recognise the need to reconcile the German national movement to the new political situation. In certain respects in 1870–1, although it was a national war and supported with great enthusiasm, the effect of the war was to reverse some of the achievements of the national and liberal movement between 1867 and 1871. This could, however, be seen as less a move back to dynastic principles than as a taking account of the way in which the predominantly Catholic population of south Germany had different values and loyalties from the dominant national movement.

The constitution of 1871 reflects much of this [32]. It was framed as an agreement between dynasties and the Reichstag deputies were excluded from the proclamation of the empire in Versailles. It allowed the retention of many vital powers by the individual states over such matters as education, direct taxation, cultural policies and welfare arrangements. Each state retained its own constitution which gave parliaments different powers in relation to the executive and where representatives on institutions such as state parliaments, district and city councils were elected by different methods and franchises. The imperial government was granted only certain specific powers: declaring war and making peace, commanding the armed forces, conducting diplomatic relations, administering the customs system. Much that touched the everyday lives of most Germans continued to be the affair of the individual state.

Not much emphasis was placed upon national values or symbols in the new empire. There was no official national anthem. (That had to wait until 1922.) There was a national flag but it is first mentioned in article 55: 'The flag of the navy and the merchant shipping is black-white-red' [32: *138*]. The flag, in other words, was introduced as a pragmatic necessity: one had to have something to fly on ships, consulates and embassies.

The most obvious national symbols clashed with dynastic principles. The national colours of black, red and gold were the colours of a nationalism which in 1848–9 had challenged the dynasties. Bismarck in his reminiscences recalls how in 1848 he led peasants in resisting the demand to put a black-red-gold flag on their church tower and instead got them to run up the Prussian colours. Later he quotes a poem which counterposes the Prussian black and white against the German black, red and gold [226: *31, 45–6*]. The colours chosen in 1871 for the national flag were black, red and white – an uneasy compromise between Prussian and German symbols.

The song *Deutschland, Deutschland über alles* had originated as an assertion of German nationality over the particular dynasties, not an assertion of German power over other nationalities. It was understandably not chosen as the national anthem but rather the (unofficial) choice fell upon the Prussian war hymn sung to the tune of *Deutschland, Deutschland über alles*. The main anniversary of the

111

Second Empire was not the day of its proclamation but rather the celebration of the victory of Sedan; making war and power the defining features of the new state. This is hardly surprising. William was present at the battlefields of Sadowa and Sedan, often within reach of enemy fire. For him the new state was quite palpably a military achievement. Later William and Bismarck themselves provided much of the political symbolism of the Second Empire. Bismarck memorials sprang up throughout Germany, especially after his death. (The classic study of these issues is Schieder [214].)

That is not to say that there was nothing national about the new state. The overwhelming majority of its subjects were German in the double sense of belonging to the territory of the German Confederation and speaking German as their first language. Even when many rejected the particular symbols of the Second Empire, for example celebrating the March insurrection of 1848 in preference to the battle of Sedan, they did so as Germans.

The *Bund* and the *Zollverein* had provided powerful unifying political and economic experiences. State identity in certain respects was fragile and artificial. After all, Bavaria, Baden and Württemberg had themselves only been created by Napoleon and confirmed by international agreement in 1814–15. Prussia also was a constantly changing entity with strong differences between the 'oldest' subjects – Brandenburgers and Prussians – the 'youngest' who had become Prussian in 1867, and many who were somewhere in between. How long does it take for someone to acquire the sense that they 'belong' to this or that state, this or that country? The Second Empire was to continue the story of reshaping the political identity of subjects which the new states of the Confederation had started. However, there was a certain unity of culture, political and economic relations that was lacking in other new states formed in zones which the old imperial powers, above all the Habsburg and Ottoman empires, could no longer control. Even in 1815 Metternich had never suggested that Germany was simply a geographical expression as he did with reference to Italy. D'Azeglio's famous dictum: 'We have made Italy, now we must make Italians' could not be applied to Germany.

So it was a kind of a national state that was formed in 1871. Its formation was not inevitable but one possible way in which the politics of Germany could have adjusted to the pressures tending to the creation of territorial, sovereign states under the conditions of modern politics. If, however, there was to be just one German state then the overwhelming likelihood was that this would be a Prussian-dominated state. The particular form that state took equally was not predetermined. It required appropriate conditions in Europe and in Germany. It required the violent exclusion of Austria from Germany by Prussia, something which few contemporaries had thought either desirable or possible. After 1867 the likelihood was that the south German states would by one means or another have been drawn into the orbit of the North German Confederation, but the fact that this came about by means of war with France gave a special character to their incorporation into Germany. The crucial decisions, above all those taken by Bismarck, were informed by a sense of the importance of nationality in modern German politics but were driven by the desire to extend Prussian power. In 1871 the new state only hesitantly and ambiguously asserted claims of national identity and loyalty over its subjects. The age of mass nationalism had not yet arrived. That was a consequence, not a cause of the new German nation-state.

Bibliography

The first part of this bibliography refers to English-language works which I think could be of especial use to students who wish to take their study of this subject further. I have kept this very short.

The second part of the bibliography consists of all the other literature cited in the text. This is simply divided into English- and German-language sections. Where appropriate, I have made a brief comment.

The third part of the bibliography provides references to works which can supply further reading and material such as maps, statistics, political data and documents.

PART A: BRIEF ANNOTATED GUIDE

Chapter 1 Historical Judgements

[1] G. Iggers, *The German Conception of History* (Middletown, Conneticut, 1969). Outline of the dominant approaches in German historical writing since the late eighteenth century.

[2] H. Böhme (ed.), *The Foundation of the German Empire: Select Documents*, trans. Agatha Ramm (Oxford, 1971). The introduction and the documents together provide a nice introduction to differing attitudes of contemporaries to German unification.

[3] H. von Treitschke, *Deutsche Geschichte im 19. Jahrhundert*, 5 vols (Leipzig, 1879–1894; Königstein, 1981). There is a 7-volume translation into English (London, 1915–19). This still reads well and is a classic representation of the 'Prussian' approach to German history. However, it is unfinished and only reaches the eve of the 1848 revolutions.

[4] H. Friedjung, *Der Kampf um die Vorherrschaft in Deutschland 1859 bis 1866*, 2 vols (Vienna, 1897); an abridged English translation by A. J. P. Taylor and W. L. McElwee of the 1916–17 edition appeared in one volume under the title *The Struggle for Supremacy in Germany 1859–1866* (London, 1935; reissued New York, 1966) with an introduction by A. J. P. Taylor. This is the work cited in the text. One of

the great studies of the conflict between Austria and Prussia, written by a liberal Austrian who admired Bismarck but deplored his achievement. But see also [5].

[5] R. Austensen, 'Austria and the "struggle for supremacy in Germany", 1848–1864', *Journal of Modern History*, 52 (1980), 192–225. An up-to-date consideration of the kind of approach taken by Friedjung.

[6] A. Dorpalen, *German History in Marxist Perspective: The East German Approach* (London, 1985). Survey of the way marxist historians of the German Democratic Republic have written about German history.

[7] H.-U. Wehler, *The German Empire 1871–1918* (Leamington Spa, 1985). Classic, if dated, example of the critical approach towards German history taken by some historians of the Federal Republic of Germany. This is taken to task by [8].

[8] D. Blackbourn & G. Eley, *The Peculiarities of German History: Bourgeois Society and Politics in Nineteenth-century Germany* (Oxford, 1984). An important critique of the 'critical' approach to modern German history.

[9] J. Sheehan, 'What is German history? Reflections on the role of the nation in German history and historiography', *Journal of Modern History*, 53/1 (1981), 1–23. A thoughtful consideration of the ways in which modern German history has been viewed through national spectacles.

Chapter 2 Conditions

General European histories

[10] E. Hobsbawm, *The Age of Revolution* (New York, 1962); *The Age of Capital* (London, 1975); and *The Age of Empire* (London, 1987). In my view this trilogy remains the finest introduction to the history of Europe between 1789 and 1914.

[11] A. Millward & K. Saul, *The Economic Development of Continental Europe 1780–1870* (London, 1973). An authoritative introduction to the economic history of Europe in this period.

[12] P. W. Schroeder, *The Transformation of European Politics 1763–1848* (Oxford, 1994). A major new publication which takes the ideological factor in foreign policy seriously and is sceptical of 'balance of power' approaches, unlike the volume in the series written 40 years earlier, namely [13].

[13] A. J. P. Taylor, *The Struggle for Mastery in Europe 1848–1918* (Oxford, 1954). The major general study of the diplomacy of the period, although now rather dated.

[14] M. Mann, *The Sources of Social Power. Vol. II The Rise of Classes and Nation-states, 1760–1914* (Cambridge, 1993). A general work

of historical sociology which seeks to show how ideological, economic, military and political forms of power combine together to shape society and state in Europe and the USA over the 'long nineteenth century'. Has some very fine chapters on the German aspect. Amongst other things it is critical of the 'realist' approach of [15].

[15] P. Kennedy, *The Rise and Fall of the Great Powers: Economic Change and Military Conflict from 1500 to 2000* (London, 1988). A general work which relates changes in power status to 'underlying' shifts in the economic balance of power.

General histories of Germany

[16] J. Sheehan, *German History 1770–1866* (Oxford, 1989). A superb general history which seeks to keep open non-Prussian perspectives on German history in this period. This is the first book to which students should turn for any aspect of the subject up to the Austro-Prussian war of 1866 and its immediate aftermath.

[17] G. Craig, *Germany 1866–1945* (Oxford, 1978). Published in the same series as [16] this remains the major textbook for the period. Especially strong on political and military history.

[18/19] T. Hamerow, *The Social Foundations of German Unification 1858–1871: Vol. 1 Ideas and Institutions* (New Jersey, 1969); *Vol. 2 Struggles and Accomplishments* (New Jersey, 1972). These two studies are packed with information and take a thematic approach to the subject; generally Prussia, liberalism and modernity are seen to be in league with one another in bringing about national unification.

Chapter 3 Processes

[20] W. Carr, *The Wars of German Unification* (London, 1991). Focuses on war and diplomacy and is a good, recent introduction to the subject.

[21] W. E. Mosse, *The European Great Powers and the German Question 1848–1871* (Cambridge, 1958). Still an authoritative study, especially for British and Russian policy.

[22] F. R. Bridge, *The Habsburg Monarchy among the Great Powers 1815–1918* (Oxford, 1990) A good summary of Austrian policy and action through the period.

The best way, in English, of approaching Prussian policy during the unification process, remains biographies of Bismarck.

[23] L. Gall, *Bismarck: the White Revolutionary*, 2 vols (London, 1986). This is a superb modern critical biography, full of reflection and analysis. Vol. 1 covers the period to 1871.

[24] O. Pflanze, *Bismarck and the Development of Germany: Vol. I The*

Period of Unification 1815–1871 (New Jersey, 1963). This volume has been republished in 1990 along with two further volumes taking the story from 1871 to Bismarck's death.

So far as the details of the three wars are concerned see also:

[25] L. D. Steefel, *The Schleswig-Holstein Question* (Cambridge, Mass., 1932). The classic diplomatic account.

[26] G. Craig, *The Battle of Königgrätz* (London, 1965). Still the standard and authoritative account.

[27] W. S. Halperin, 'The Origins of the Franco-Prussian war revisited: Bismarck and the Hohenzollern candidature for the Spanish throne', *Journal of Modern History*, 45 (1973), 83–91 is a useful review of the debate.

[28] M. Howard, *The Franco-Prussian War: The German Invasion of France, 1870–1871* (London, 1961). The authoritative study of the war.

It is difficult to recommend much in English (apart from [16] above) on the German dimensions to the process of unification. For a good understanding of the national movement in 1848–9 see:

[29] F. Eyck, *The Frankfurt Parliament 1848–49* (London, 1968). Best English language study of the German National Assembly of 1848–9.

For a sketch of the development of a national movement see also:

[30] D. Düding, 'The nineteenth-century German nationalist movement as a movement of societies', in H. Schulze (ed.), *Nation-building in Central Europe* (Leamington Spa, 1987), pp. 19–49. Summary of his German monograph [see 179 below] on the subject.

For a rather iconoclastic consideration of nationalism and its significance see:

[31] M. Hughes, *Nationalism and Society in Germany 1800–1945* (London, 1988). A debunking approach to the role of nationalism in modern German politics.

Chapter 4 Results

For the text of the constitution of the 1871 *Reich* (which can also conveniently be compared with that of the Imperial Constitution of 1849) see:

[32] G. Hucko (ed.), *The Democratic Tradition: Four German Constitutions* (Leamington Spa, 1987). Translations of the constitutions of 1849, 1871, 1919 and 1949.

For some thoughts on the relationship between national identity and state-building see:

[33] J. Breuilly, 'Sovereignty and boundaries: modern state formation and national identity in Germany', in *National Histories and European History*, ed. M. Fulbrook (London, 1993), pp. 94–140.

Finally, for students who wish to relate the story of German unification to the broader history of the national idea and the nation-state in modern German history, see the various essays in:

[34] J. Breuilly (ed.), *The State of Germany: the National Idea in the Making, Unmaking and Remaking of a Modern Nation-state* (London, 1992).

PART B: OTHER ENGLISH AND GERMAN WORKS CITED

English-language literature

[35] P. Adelman, *Victorian Radicalism: the Middle-class Experience 1830–1914* (London, 1984).
[36] E. N. Anderson, *The Social and Political Conflicts in Prussia 1858–1864* (Lincoln, Nebraska, 1954). Still the most detailed study in English on the nature and basis of political conflict in Prussia in this period.
[37] E. N. Anderson, 'The Prussian *Volksschule* in the nineteenth Century' in *Festschrift für Hans Rosenberg*, ed. G. A. Ritter (Berlin, 1970), pp. 261–79.
[38] C. Applegate, *A Nation of Provincials: The German Idea of Heimat* (Berkeley, CA, 1990). A subtle study of the way in which senses of identity develop and change in a particular German region.
[39] A. Arblaster, *The Rise and Decline of Western Liberalism* (Oxford, 1984).
[40] R. Austensen, 'The making of Austrian Prussian policy 1848–52', *Historical Journal*, 27 (1984), 861–76.
[41] K. Bade (ed.), *Population, Labour and Migration in Nineteenth and Twentieth Century Germany* (Leamington Spa, 1987).
[42] D. Beales, 'Garibaldi in England: the politics of Italian enthusiasm', in *Essays in Honour of D. Mack Smith*, ed. J. Davis & P. Ginsborg (Cambridge, 1990), pp. 184–216.
[43] R. Berdahl, *The Politics of the Prussian Nobility: The Development of a Conservative Ideology 1770–1848* (New Jersey, 1988). Shows how traditionalism gave way to an explicit conservative ideology of paternalism. Also useful for basic social and economic history of Prussian rural society.

118

[44] D. Blackbourn, 'The German bourgeoisie: an introduction', in [46], pp. 1–45.

[45] D. Blackbourn, *Marpingen: Apparitions of the Virgin Mary in Bismarckian Germany* (Oxford, 1993).

[46] D. Blackbourn & R. J. Evans (eds), *The German Bourgeoisie: Essays on the Social History of the German Middle Class from the late Eighteenth to the early Twentieth Century* (London, 1991).

[47] T. C. W. Blanning, *The French Revolution in Germany: Occupation and Resistance in the Rhineland, 1792–1802* (Oxford, 1983). Demonstrates the unimportance of either radical or national ideas in the Rhenish response to the French.

[48] J.-P. Bled, *Franz Joseph* (Oxford, 1994). The most up-to-date popular biography.

[49] J. Blum, *Noble Landowners and Agriculture in Austria 1815–1848: A Study in the Origins of the Peasant Emancipation of 1848* (Baltimore, 1948). Argues reform went in direction desired by noble landowners wishing to farm in a more capitalist manner.

[50] J. Blum, *The End of the Old Order in Rural Europe* (New Jersey, 1978).

[51] G. Bonin, *Bismarck and the Hohenzollern Candidature for the Spanish Throne: The Documents in the German Diplomatic Archives* (London, 1957).

[52] K. Borchardt, *The Industrial Revolution in Germany 1700–1914*, Vol. 4/Section 4 of *The Fontana Economic History of Europe* (London, 1972).

[53] K. Bourne, *The Foreign Policy of Victorian England, 1832–1902* (Oxford, 1970).

[54] J. Breuilly, 'Nations and nationalism in modern German history', *The Historical Journal*, 33/3 (1990), 659–75.

[55] J. Breuilly, 'The national idea in modern German history', in [34], pp. 1–28.

[56] J. Breuilly, 'State-building, modernisation and liberalism from the late eighteenth century to unification: German peculiarities', *European History Quarterly*, 22 (1992), 257–84.

[57] J. Breuilly, *Nationalism and the State* (2nd edn, Manchester, 1993).

[58] F. R. Bridge, *From Sadowa to Sarajevo: The Foreign Policy of Austria-Hungary, 1866–1914* (London, 1972). The most detailed study of post-1866 Austrian foreign policy.

[59] P. Brock, 'Polish democrats and the English radicals 1832–1862: a chapter in the history of Anglo-Polish relations', *Journal of Modern History*, 25 (1953), 139–56.

[60] E. D. Brose, *The Politics of Technological Change in Prussia: Out of the Shadow of Antiquity, 1809–1848* (New Jersey, 1993). Shows

119

how a new conception of the economy developed amongst Prussian elites.

[61] R. Brubacker, *Citizenship and Nationhood in France and Germany* (London, 1992). A pioneering work on the development of modern forms of citizenship and their links to nationality.

[62] A. Bucholz, *Moltke, Schlieffen and Prussian War Planning* (Oxford, 1991). Applies concepts of management to military history.

[63] M. Burleigh, *Germany Turns Eastwards: a Study of Ostforschung in the Third Reich* (Cambridge, 1988).

[64] W. Carr, *Schleswig-Holstein, 1815–1848: a Study in National Conflict* (London, 1963). Shows how national affiliations develop.

[65] W. Carr, 'The Unification of Germany', in [34], pp. 80–102. Short summary of arguments of [20].

[66] F. Carsten, *A History of the Prussian Junkers* (Aldershot, 1989).

[67] L. M. Case, *French Opinion on War and Diplomacy during the Second Empire* (Philadelphia, 1954).

[68] G. Claeys, 'Mazzini, Kossuth and British Radicalism, 1848–1854', *Journal of British Studies*, 28 (1989), 225–61.

[69] C. W. Clark, *Franz Joseph and Bismarck: The Diplomacy of Austria before the War of 1866* (Cambridge, 1934).

[70] G. Cohen, *The Politics of Ethnic Survival: Germans in Prague, 1861–1914* (New Jersey, 1981). Shows how a sense of Bohemian identity gave way to conceptions of conflicting German and Czech identities.

[71] G. Craig, *The Politics of the Prussian Army 1640–1945* (New York, 1964).

[72] G. Craig, *The Triumph of Liberalism: Zürich in the Golden Age 1830–1869* (London, 1988).

[73] I. Cummins, *Marx, Engels and National Movements* (London, 1980).

[74] J. A. Davis, *Conflict and Control: Law and Order in Nineteenth-Century Italy* (London, 1988).

[75] J. R. Davis, Trade, Politics, Perspectives, and the Question of a British Commercial Policy towards the German states 1848–1866 (PhD, University of Glasgow, 1994).

[76] I. Deak, *The Lawful Revolution: Louis Kossuth and the Hungarians, 1848–49* (New York, 1979).

[77] I. Deak, *Beyond Nationalism: a Social and Political History of the Habsburg Officer Corps 1848–1918* (Oxford, 1992).

[78] R. Dominick, Wilhelm Liebknecht and German Social Democracy, 1869–1900 (PhD, University of North Carolina, 1973). This has since been published as a book under the title of *Wilhelm Liebknecht and the Founding of the German Social Democratic Party* (Chapel Hill, NC, 1982).

[79] B. Elrod, 'Bernhard von Rechberg and the Metternichian tradition:

the dilemmas of conservative statecraft', *Journal of Modern History*, 56 (Sept. 1984), 430–55.

[80] K. Epstein, *The Genesis of German Conservatism* (New Jersey, 1966).

[81] E. Eyck, *Bismarck and the German Empire* (London, 1950). A classic study written from a liberal viewpoint.

[82] F. Fischer, *From Kaiserreich to Third Reich: Elements of Continuity in German History, 1871–1945* (London, 1986).

[83] E. Gellner, *Nations and Nationalism* (London, 1983).

[84] D. F. Good, *The Economic Rise of the Habsburg Empire, 1750–1914* (Berkeley, CA, 1984).

[85] L. Greenfeld, *Nationalism: Five Roads to Modernity* (Cambridge, Mass., 1992). The chapter on Germany takes the view of German nationalism as essentially ethnic and having deep roots in the German past.

[86] M. Greengrass (ed.), *Conquest and Coalescence: the Shaping of the State in Early Modern Europe* (London, 1991). Interesting studies of how particular regions are added to a state, worth comparing with the way in which Prussia added other states to herself to make Germany.

[87] C. W. Hallberg, *Franz Joseph and Napoleon III 1852–1864: a Study of Austro-French Relations* (New York, 1973). Stresses the ideological differences between the leaders and their regimes which prevented a positive understanding.

[88] T. Hamerow, *Restoration, Revolution, Reaction: Economics and Politics in Germany, 1815–1871* (New Jersey, 1958).

[89] T. Hamerow, '1848', in *The Responsibility of Power*, ed. L. Krieger & F. Stern (New York, 1967), pp. 145–61.

[90] J. F. Harris, *A Study in the Theory and Practice of German Liberalism: Eduard Lasker, 1829–1884* (New York, 1984).

[91] H. Hearder, *Italy in the Age of the Risorgimento 1790–1870* (London, 1983).

[92] W. O. Henderson, *The Zollverein* (2nd edn, London, 1968). English language treatment, largely narrative and seeing a national significance in the customs union from the outset.

[93] W. O. Henderson, *Friedrich List: Economist and Visionary, 1789–1846* (London, 1983).

[94] E. Hobsbawm, *Nations and Nationalism since 1780: Programme, Myth, Reality* (2nd edn, Cambridge, 1992).

[95] E. Hobsbawm & T. Ranger (eds), *The Invention of Tradition* (2nd edn, Cambridge, 1992).

[96] S. L. Hochstadt, 'Migration in Preindustrial Germany', *Central European History*, 16 (1983), 195–224. Critical of stereotypes of premodern society as a rooted, immobile society, though that might still be largely the case for the first half of the nineteenth century.

[97] N. Hope, *The Alternative to German Unification: The Anti-Prussian*

Party, Frankfurt, Nassau and the two Hessen 1859–1867 (Wiesbaden, 1973). Major English-language study giving details on views of medium states and the *großdeutsch* movement.

[98] T. F. Huertas, *Economic Growth and Economic Policy in a Multinational Setting: The Habsburg Monarchy, 1841–1865* (New York, 1977).

[99] M. Hughes, *Early Modern Germany 1477–1806* (London, 1992).

[100] M. Hughes, 'Fiat justitia, pereat Germania? The imperial supreme jurisdiction and imperial reform in the later Holy Roman Empire', in [34], pp. 29–46.

[101] B. Jelavich, *Modern Austria: Empire and Republic 1815–1986* (Cambridge, 1987).

[102] M. John, 'Between estate and profession: lawyers and the development of the legal profession in nineteenth-century Germany', in [46], pp. 162–97.

[103] L. E. Jones & J. N. Retallack (eds), *Between Reform, Reaction and Resistance: Studies in the History of German Conservatism from 1789 to 1945* (Oxford, 1993).

[104] R. Kann, *The Multi-National Empire: nationalism and national reform in the Habsburg monarchy, 1848–1918*, 2 vols (New York, 1950). Vol. 1 outlines situations and events; Vol. 2 focuses on policies and personalities.

[105] P. Katzenstein, *Disjoined Partners: Austria and Germany since 1815* (Berkeley, CA, 1976). An ambitious attempt to use political concepts, above all to do with communications, to understand Austro-Prussian relations.

[106] E. Kedourie, *Nationalism* (3rd edn, London, 1966).

[107] E. Kehr, *Battleship Building and Party Politics in Germany* (Chicago, 1975).

[108] E. Kehr, *Economic Interest, Militarism and Foreign Policy: Essays on German History* (Berkeley, CA, 1977).

[109] T. Kemp, *Industrialisation in Nineteenth-century Europe* (London, 1969).

[110] H. Kiesewetter, 'Economic Preconditions for Germany's Nation Building in the Nineteenth Century', in H. Schulze (ed.), *Nationbuilding in Central Europe* (Leamington Spa, 1987), pp. 81–106. Emphasises the sea change that came around mid-century.

[111] E. Kraehe, 'Austria and the Problem of Reform in the German Confederation, 1851–1863', *American Historical Review*, 56 (1950/51), 276–94.

[112] E. Kraehe, *Metternich's German Policy: Vol. II The Congress of Vienna 1814–1815* (New Jersey, 1983).

[113] W. Langer, *Political and Social Upheaval 1832–1852* (New York, 1969).

[114] D. Langewiesche, 'Germany and the national question in 1848', in [34], pp. 60–79.

[115] W. Langsam, *The Napoleonic Wars and German Nationalism in Austria* (New York, 1930).

[116] A. Lees, *Revolution and Reflection: Intellectual Change in Germany during the 1850s* (The Hague, 1974).

[117] L. Lloyd, *The Politics of Harmony: Civil Service, Liberalism and Social Reform in Baden 1800–1850* (Newark, 1980).

[118] C. A. Macartney, *The Habsburg Empire 1790–1918* (London, 1968).

[119] R. Magraw, *France 1815–1914: The Bourgeois Century* (Oxford, 1983).

[120] Karl Marx & Friedrich Engels, *Selected Works in One Volume* (Moscow, 1968).

[121] M. Maynes, *Schooling for the People: France and Germany, 1750–1850* (New York, 1985).

[122] C. McClelland, *State, Society and University in Germany, 1700–1914* (Cambridge, 1980).

[123] W. H. McNeill, *The Pursuit of Power: Technology, Armed Force, and Society since AD 1000* (Oxford, 1983).

[124] R. Millman, *British Foreign Policy and the Coming of the Franco-Prussian War* (Oxford, 1965).

[125] A. Millward & K. B. Saul, *The Development of the Economies of Continental Europe 1850–1914* (London, 1977).

[126] G. L. Mosse, *The Nationalisation of the Masses* (New York, 1975).

[127] D. T. Murphy, 'Prussian aims for the *Zollverein*, 1828–1833', *The Historian*, 53 (1991), 283–302.

[128] L. B. Namier, *1848: the Revolution of the Intellectuals* (London, 1944). A hostile treatment of the 'liberals' of the German National Assembly.

[129] H. Nicolson, *The Congress of Vienna: A Study in Allied Unity 1815–1822* (New York, 1946).

[130] P. Noyes, *Organisation and Revolution: Working-class Associations in the German Revolutions of 1848–49* (New Jersey, 1966).

[131] F. Ohles, *Germany's Rude Awakening: Censorship in the Land of the Brothers Grimm* (Kent, Ohio, 1992).

[132] Open University, *A321: The Revolutions of 1848* (Milton Keynes, 1976).

[133] S. Pech, *The Czech Revolution of 1848* (Chapel Hill, NC, 1969).

[134] P. Pilbeam, *Republicanism in France* (London, 1994).

[135] S. Pollard, *Peaceful Conquest: The Industrialization of Europe 1760–1970* (Oxford, 1981).

[136] B. Porter, *The Refugee Question in mid-Victorian Politics* (Cambridge, 1979).

[137] E. A. Pottinger, *Napoleon III and the German Crisis 1865–1866* (Cambridge, Mass., 1966). Argues that a pro-Prussian sentiment was important in shaping Napoleon's policies between the Convention of Gastein and the outbreak of war, although his calculations were upset by the victory at Königgrätz.

[138] J. Rath, *The Viennese Revolution of 1848* (Austin, TX, 1957).

[139] G. de Ruggiero, *The History of European Liberalism* (Boston, 1959).

[140] K. Schleunes, *Schooling and Society: The Politics of Education in Prussia and Bavaria 1750–1900* (Oxford, 1989).

[141] H. Schmitt, 'From Sovereign States to Prussian Provinces: Hanover and Hesse-Nassau 1866–71', *Journal of Modern History*, 57/1 (1985), 24–56. How Prussia effectively incorporated these territories in ways which blunted dogmatic centralising drive from Berlin. Interesting on issues concerning domain and other 'private' revenues of the rulers of these states. Also shows how areas became National Liberal strongholds.

[142] H. Schmitt, 'Count Beust and Germany, 1866–70: reconquest, realignment, or resignation', *Central European History*, 1 (1968), 20–34.

[143] P. W. Schroeder, 'Europe and the German Confederation in the 1860s', in [212], pp. 281–91.

[144] H. Schulze, *The Course of German Nationalism: From Frederick the Great to Bismarck 1763–1867* (Cambridge, 1991). A useful overview of the subject with some documents.

[145] H. Schulze (ed.), *Nation-Building in Central Europe* (Leamington Spa, 1987). Some useful essays on various conditions of German unification.

[146] J. Sheehan, *German Liberalism in the Nineteenth Century* (Chicago, 1978). The best English language account.

[147] J. Sheehan, 'State and nationality in the Napoleonic period', in [34], pp. 47–59.

[148] D. Showalter, *Railroads and Rifles: Soldiers, Technology and the Unification of Germany* (Hamden, CT, 1986). A fine study of how railways and weapons were integrated into military policy.

[149] A. Sked, *The Survival of the Habsburg Empire: Radetzky, the Imperial Army and the Class War 1848* (London, 1979).

[150] J. Snell, *The Democratic Movement in Germany 1789–1914*, ed. and completed H. A. Schmitt (Chapel Hill, NC, 1976).

[151] J. Sperber, *Popular Catholicism in Nineteenth-Century Germany* (New Jersey, 1984).

[152] J. Sperber, *Rhineland Radicals: The Democratic Movement and the Revolution of 1848–49* (New Jersey, 1991).

[153] J. Sperber, 'Festivals of National Unity in the German Revolution of 1848–49', *Past and Present*, 136 (1992), 114–38.

[154] J. Sperber, *The European Revolutions, 1848–1851* (Cambridge, 1994).

[155] L. D. Steefel, *Bismarck, the Hohenzollern Candidacy and the Origins of the German War of 1870* (Cambridge, Mass., 1962).

[156] H. von Sybel, *The Founding of the German Empire by William I*, 7 vols (1890; reprint, New York, 1968).

[157] R. H. Thomas, *Liberalism, Nationalism and the German Intellectuals 1822–1847* (Cambridge, 1951).

[158] L. Torres, The German *Nationalverein* 1859–1867 (PhD, University of Minnesota, 1971).

[159] M. Walker, *German Home Towns: Community, State and General Estate 1648–1871* (London, 1971).

[160] E. Weber, *Peasants into Frenchmen: the Modernisation of Rural France, 1870–1914* (London, 1977).

[161] D. White, *The Splintered Party: National Liberalism in Hessen and the Reich 1867–1918* (Cambridge, Mass., 1976).

[162] J. R. Wilson, *Seedbed of Protest: Social Structure and Radical Politics in Ettlingen, Grand Duchy of Baden, 1815–1850* (New York, 1992).

[163] G. Windell, *The Catholics and German Unity 1861–1871* (Minneapolis, 1954).

[164] D. Wright, *Popular Radicalism: the Working Class Experience 1780–1880* (London, 1988).

[165] T. Zeldin, *The Political System of Napoleon III* (London, 1958).

[166] S. Zucker, *Ludwig Bamberger: German Liberal Politician and Social Critic, 1823–1899* (Pittsburgh, PA, 1975).

German-language literature

[167] R. Aldenhoff, *Schulze-Delitzsch. Ein Beitrag zur Geschichte des Liberalismus zwischen Revolution und Reichsgründung* (Bonn, 1984).

[168] K. O. v. Aretin, *Heiliges Römisches Reich 1776 bis 1806: Reichsverfassung und Staatssouveränität*, 2 vols (Wiesbaden, 1967).

[169] H. Bartels & E. Engelberg (eds), *Die großpreußisch-militarische Reichsgründung 1871: Voraussetzungen und Folgen* (Berlin, 1971).

[170] H. Baumgarten, *Der deutsche Liberalismus: eine Selbstkritik* (orig. pub. 1866; ed. A. Birke, Frankfurt/M., 1974).

[171] H. Berding & H.-P. Ullmann (eds), *Deutschland zwischen Revolution und Restauration* (Königstein/Ts., 1981).

[172] H. Berding, 'Die Entstehung des Deutschen Zollvereins als Problem historischer Forschung', in *Vom Ancien régime zum modernen Parteienstaat. Festschrift für Theodor Schieder* (Munich & Vienna, 1978), pp. 225–37.

[173] W. Blessing, *Staat und Kirche in der Gesellschaft. Institutioneller*

Autorität und mentaler Wandel in Bayern während des 19. Jahrhunderts (Göttingen, 1982).

[174] R. Boch, *Grenzenloses Wachstum? Das rheinische Wirtschaftsbürgertum und seine Industrialisierungsdebatte 1814–1857* (Göttingen, 1991). Like Brose [60] interesting on changing conceptions of the economy.

[175] H. Böhme, *Deutschlands Weg zur Grossmacht. Studien zum Verhältnis von Wirtschaft und Staat während der Reichsgründungszeit 1848–1881* (3rd edn, Cologne, 1974). The major study emphasising economic factors, especially to do with the *Zollverein*, in bringing about German unification.

[176] W. Conze & D. Groh, *Die Arbeiterbewegung in der nationalen Bewegung* (Stuttgart, 1977).

[177] A. Doering-Manteuffel, 'Der Ordnungszwang des Staatensystems: Zu den Mitteleuropa-Konzepten in der österreichisch-preußischen Rivalität 1849–1851', in A. M. Birke & G. Heydemann (eds), *Die Herausforderung des Europäischen Staatensystems* (Göttingen, 1989), pp. 119–40.

[178] A. Doering-Manteuffel, *Die deutsche Frage und das europäische Staatensystem 1815–1871* (Munich, 1993).

[179] D. Düding, *Organisierter gesellschaftlicher Nationalismus in Deutschland (1808–1847). Bedeutung und Funktion der Türner- und Sängervereine für die deutsche Nationalbewegung* (Munich, 1984).

[180] D. Düding et al. (eds), *Öffentliche Festkultur: Politische Feste in Deutschland von der Aufklärung bis zum Ersten Weltkrieg* (Reinbek bei Hamburg, 1988).

[181] R. Dumke, 'Der deutsche Zollverein als Modell ökonomischer Integration', in H. Berding (ed.), *Wirtschaftliche und politische Integration in Europa im 19. und 20 Jahrhundert* (Göttingen, 1984), pp. 72–101. Along with Berding [172] casts doubt on the 'national' mission of the *Zollverein*.

[182] R. Dumke, 'Anglo-deutscher Handel und Frühindustrialisierung in Deutschland 1822–1860', *Geschichte und Gesellschaft*, V (1979), 175–200. Develops the idea of a triangular trade flow pattern.

[183] E. Engelberg, *Bismarck: Urpreuße und Reichsgründer* (Berlin, 1985). A massive labour of love; very traditional and positive given its official marxist status. Engelberg has since published the sequel *Bismarck: Das Reich in der Mitte Europas* (Berlin, 1990) taking the story from 1871 to the end of Bismarck's life.

[184] R. Engelsing, *Analphabetum und Lektüre. Zur Sozialgeschichte des Lesens in Deutschland* (Stuttgart, 1973).

[185] B. Faulenbach, *Ideologie des deutschen Weges. Die deutsche Geschichte in der Historiographie zwischen Kaiserreich und Nationalsozialismus* (Munich, 1980).

[186] H. Freudenthal, *Vereine in Hamburg* (Hamburg, 1968).

[187] W. Gruner, *Die deutsche Frage. Ein Problem der europäischen Geschichte seit 1800* (Munich, 1985).

[188] H.-W. Hahn, *Geschichte des Deutschen Zollvereins* (Göttingen, 1984). The most recent general account.

[189] H.-W. Hahn, 'Mitteleuropäische oder kleindeutsche Wirtschaftsordnung in der Epoche des Deutschen Bundes' in [212], pp. 186–214.

[190] M. Hettling & P. Nolte (eds), *Bürgerliche Feste: Symbolische Formen politischen Handelns im 19. Jahrhundert* (Göttingen, 1993).

[191] G. Heydemann, 'Philhellenismus in Deutschland und Großbritannien', in [177], pp. 31–60.

[192] M. Jeismann, *Das Vaterland der Feinde: Studien zum nationalen Feindbegriff und Selbstverständnis in Deutschland und Frankreich 1792–1918* (Stuttgart, 1992).

[193] S. Kienewicz, 'Die Polenbegeisterung in Westeuropa', in [177], pp. 61–75.

[194] E. Kolb, *Der Kriegsausbruch 1870. Politische Entscheidungsprozesse und Verantwortlichkeiten in der Julikrise 1870* (Göttingen, 1970).

[195] E. Kolb (ed.), *Europa vor dem Krieg von 1870: Mächte Konstellation – Konfliktsfelde – Kriegsausbruch* (Munich, 1987). The most recent detailed consideration of the origins of the war of 1870.

[196] M. Kraul, *Das deutsche Gymnasium 1780–1980* (Frankfurt/M., 1984).

[197] D. Langewiesche, *Liberalismus in Deutschland* (Frankfurt/M., 1988). The best German language account of the subject.

[198] D. Langewiesche, *Republik und Republikaner. Von der historischen Entwertung eines politischen Begriffs* (Stuttgart, 1993).

[199] H. Lutz, *Zwischen Habsburg und Preussen. Deutschland 1815–1866* (Berlin, 1985). Seeks deliberately to avoid seeing events from the Prussian perspective and largely succeeds.

[200] W. Mommsen, *Stein, Ranke, Bismarck. Ein Beitrag zur politischen und sozialen Bewegung des 19. Jahrhunderts* (Munich, 1954). A pioneering study of the meaning of terms like Germany and nation in the thinking of these three Germans.

[201] S. Na'aman, *Der deutsche Nationalverein. Die politische Konstituierung des deutschen Bürgertums 1859–1867* (Düsseldorf, 1987). The most detailed recent account, especially good on the political culture of the period.

[202] T. Nipperdey, 'Nationalidee und Nationaldenkmal in Deutschland im 19. Jahrhundert', in Nipperdey, *Gesellschaft, Kultur, Theorie: Gesammelte Aufsätze zur neueren Geschichte* (Göttingen, 1976), pp. 133–74.

[203] T. Nipperdey, 'Wehlers Gesellschaftsgeschichte', *Geschichte und Gesellschaft*, 14 (1988), 403–15.

[204] T. Nipperdey, *Deutsche Geschichte*, 3 vols (Munich, 1983, 1990, 1992). This is one of the major general histories of nineteenth-century Germany. The first volume was published under the title *Deutsche Geschichte 1800–1866: Bürgerwelt und starker Staat*. The second volume was *Deutsche Geschichte 1866–1918: Bd. I. Arbeitswelt und Bürgergeist*, and the third *Deutsche Geschichte 1866–1918. Bd. II. Machtstaat vor der Demokratie*. For the approach of this work see the following English language review articles [205, 206].

[205] J. Breuilly, '"Telling it as it was?": Thomas Nipperdey's history of nineteenth-century Germany', *History*, 80/258 (February, 1995), 59–70.

[206] J. Sperber, 'Master Narratives of Nineteenth-century German History', *Central European History*, 24/1 (1991), 69–91. A review of three recent general histories of nineteenth-century Germany by Nipperdey [204], Sheehan [16] and Wehler [221].

[207] R. Noltenius, 'Schiller als Führer und Heiland. Das Schillerfest 1859 als nationaler Traum von der Geburt des zweiten deutschen Kaiserreichs', in [180], pp. 237–58.

[208] R. Postel, *Johann Martin Lappenberg. Ein Beitrag zur Geschichte der Geschichtswissenschaft im 19. Jahrhundert* (Lübeck & Hamburg, 1972). An example of the connection between local history and conservative views of German nationality.

[209] G. Ritter, *Die preußische Konservativen und Bismarcks deutsche Politik 1858 bis 1876* (Heidelberg, 1913).

[210] G. Ritter, *Stein. Eine politische Biographie* (Stuttgart, 1981).

[211] H. Rumpler, *Die deutsche Politik des Freiherrn von Beust 1848– 1850: Zur Problematik mittelstaatlicher Reformpolitik im Zeitalter der Paulskirche* (Vienna, 1972).

[212] H. Rumpler (ed.), *Deutsche Bund und deutsche Frage 1815–1866* (Munich, 1990). A series of essays which considers the positive aspects of the German *Bund*.

[213] R. Schenda, *Volk ohne Buch. Studien zur Sozialgeschichte der populären Lesestoffe* (Frankfurt/M., 1970).

[214] T. Schieder, *Der deutsche Kaiserreich von 1871 als Nationalstaat* (Cologne & Opladen, 1961). A pioneering study of what it means to call the *Reich* of 1871 a nation-state.

[215] F. Schnabel, *Deutsche Geschichte im 19. Jahrhundert*, 4 vols (Freiburg, 1929–37; Munich, 1987). Like von Treitschke, an unfinished history of nineteenth-century Germany; unlike von Treitschke stresses non-Prussian perspectives.

[216] W. Siemann, *Die deutsche Revolution von 1848–49* (Frankfurt/M., 1985). Best recent account of the 1848–49 revolutions in the German lands.

[217] W. Siemann 'Wandel der Politik – Wandel der Staatsgewalt. Der Deutsche Bund in der Spannung zwischen "Gesammt-Macht" und "völkerrechtlichem Verein"', in [212], pp. 59–73.

[218] H. von. Srbik, *Deutsche Einheit. Idee und Wirklichkeit von Heiligen Reich bis Königgrätz*, 4 vols (Munich, 1935–42). An Austrian historian who does not see things from the Prussian point of view.

[219] R. Stadelman & W. Fischer, *Die Bildungswelt des deutschen Handwerkers um 1800* (Berlin, 1955).

[220] V. Valentin, *Geschichte der deutschen Revolution von 1848–49*, 2 vols (1930–1; pbk edn, Berlin, 1970). The classic liberal interpretation of the revolutions.

[221] H.-U. Wehler, *Deutsche Gesellschaftsgeschichte. Vol. II Von der Reformära bis zur industriellen und politischen 'Deutsche Doppelrevolution', 1815–1845/49* (Munich, 1987). Second volume of a major 'societal' history of Germany: for detailed reviews in English see above [206] and also [222].

[222] J. Breuilly, 'Wehler's Gesellschaftsgeschichte', *German History. Journal of the German History Society*, 9/2 (June 1991), 211–30.

PART C: DOCUMENTS, STATISTICS, HANDBOOKS, BIBLIOGRAPHIES

Documents

[223] Historische Reichskommission (ed.), *Die auswärtige Politik Preussens 1858–1871* (Munich, 1932–45), 9 vols.

[224] Bismarck, Otto von, *Werke in Auswahl*, 8 vols (Darmstadt, 1962–80), ed. G. Rein et al.

[225] Bismarck, *Gesammelte Werke*, 15 parts in 19 vols (Berlin, 1924–35).

[226] Bismarck, *Gedanken und Erinnerungen* (Berlin, 1990) with an introduction by Lothar Gall.

[227] A full translation of [226] under the title *Bismarck: The Man and the Statesman* was published in two volumes in 1899 (London and New York). I have used the German work but give parallel references to the translation.

[228] T. Hamerow (ed.), *The Age of Bismarck: Documents and Interpretations* (New York, 1973).

[229] H. C. Meyer (ed.), *Mitteleuropa in German Thought and Action, 1815–1945* (The Hague, 1955).

129

Statistics

[230] B. R. Mitchell, *European Historical Statistics 1750–1970* (abridged edn, London, 1978).
[231] W. Fischer et al. (eds), *Sozialgeschichtliches Arbeitsbuch I. Materialien zur Statistik des deutschen Bundes 1815–1870* (Munich, 1982).
[232] P. Bairoch, 'International industrialisation levels from 1750 to 1980', *Journal of European Economic History*, 1 (1982), 269–333.
[233] B. R. Mitchell, 'Statistical Appendix', in C. Cipolla (ed.), *The Fontana Economic History of Europe: The Emergence of Industrial Societies – 2* (London, 1973), pp. 738–820.
[234] P. Flora (ed.), *State, Economy and Society in Western Europe 1815–1975: A Data Handbook*, vol. 1 (London, 1983).
[235] B. R. Mitchell, *European Historical Statistics 1750–1980* (unabridged edn, London, 1975).
[236] P. Bairoch, 'Europe's gross national product 1800–1975', *Journal of European Economic History*, 5 (1976), 273–340.

Handbooks (useful for political facts and institutions, etc.)

[237] C. Emsley, *The Longman Companion to Napoleonic Europe* (London, 1993).
[238] R. Pearson, *The Longman Companion to European Nationalism 1789–1920* (London, 1994).
[239] C. Cook & J. Stevenson, *The Longman Handbook of Modern European History 1763–1985* (London, 1987).
[240] J. Belchem & R. Price (eds), *A Dictionary of Nineteenth-Century World History* (Oxford, 1994).

Bibliographies

[241] J. Fout (ed.), *German History and Civilisation 1806–1914. A Bibliography of Scholarly Periodical Literature* (Metuchen, NY, 1974).
[242] H.-U. Wehler, *Bibliographie zur neueren deutschen Sozialgeschichte* (Munich, 1993). Contains some 10,000 references organised under 73 headings, some thematic and some by period.
[243] *Historical Abstracts (1775–1945)*, ed. E. Boehm (Santa Barbara, CA, 1955ff). This has now shifted from print to CD-ROM form.

There are many CD-ROM bibliographic databases which are relevant to studies of modern German history and I would advise students to consult the information services of university libraries.

Table I: Some statistical comparisons

Columns	1–3 Population (million)			4–5 Per cent of labour force in manufacturing industry		6–8 Relative share of world manufacturing output			9–10 Key outputs in 1870		11–12 Government expenditure as per cent of national output		13–15 Military manpower (millions)			16–17 Per cent of government expenditure on military		18–20 Per capita GNP (in 1960 US dollars and prices)		
	1820	1840	1870	1850	1870	1800	1830	1860	Coal	Steel	1860	1870	1816	1830	1860	1860	1870	1830	1850	1870
BRITAIN	21.8	26.6	31.4	28.0	34.2	4.3	9.5	19.9	112.2	0.3	11	7	0.25	0.14	0.35	25	32	346	458	62
FRANCE	30.5	34.2	36.1	20.6 [1850]	22.0 [1866]	4.2	5.2	7.9	13.3	0.08	9	10	0.13	0.26	0.6	39	26	264	333	43
RUSSIA	48.6	62.4	84.5	–	12.2 [1897]	5.6	5.6	7.0	0.7	0.01	–	–	0.8	0.83	0.86	–	–	170	175	25
PRUSSIA/ GERMANY	10.3 / 26.1	14.9 / 32.6	19.4 / 40.8	c. 20.0	28.0 [1882]	3.5	3.5	4.9	23.3	0.13	8	15	0.13	0.13	0.2	36	40	245	308	42
AUSTRIA-HUNGARY	25.5	–	34.8	14.8 [1857]	13.1 [1869]	3.2	3.2	4.2	6.3	0.02	11	11	0.22	0.27	0.3	51	24	250	283	30

131

Table II: Some key comparisons of the three major combatants in the wars of unification

	Austria	France	Prussia
Military			
1850	434,000	439,000	131,000
1860	306,000	608,000	201,000
1866	275,000	458,000	214,000[a]
1870	252,000	452,000	319,000[b]

Education	Primary	Secondary	Primary	Secondary	Primary[e]	Secondary
1850[c]	2,413,000	48,000	3,322,000	47,900	2,583,565	103,863
1865[d]	2,654,000	80,600	4,437,000	65,700	2,825,322	90,899

Railways (kilometres in operation)			
1850	1,579	2,915	5,856[f]
1860	4,543	9,167	11,089
1870	9,589	15,544	18,876

[a] In 1866 Italy, Prussia's ally, had an army of 233,000.
[b] By 1871 the German States under Prussia's leadership could mobilise 850,000 men.
[c] The dates are actually 1851 for France, 1854 for Austria and 1852 for Prussia.
[d] The dates are actually 1865 for Austria and France, and 1864 for Prussia.
[e] Prussian figures exclude private schools.
[f] The figures are for the territory of the 1871 *Reich*.

132

Sources used for Tables I and II

Comments

The purpose of these two tables is less to illustrate points in the text and more to provide additional information to help understanding of the process of German nation-state formation. How far can one 'read off' political-military achievements from trends in economic development, or education, transportation, the armed forces, or population, or government expenditure? I hope these statistics provide some food for thought. In particular it is worth noting shifts in the relative positions of the major powers, especially Austria, France and Prussia.

The statistics provide only very rough estimates. There is a particular problem with figures for Prussia. Many subsequent compilations 'anticipate' German unification and the pre-1871 figures are often for the territory of the 1871 *Reich* (or the *Bund* excluding Austria) rather than for contemporary Prussia.

Table I: statistical comparisons of the five major European powers: sources used

1. Population figures (cols 1–3)
   Austria: [16:*459*].
   France: [230:4].
   Prussia: [16:*459* (cols 1 & 2); 231:*22* (col.2)].
   Germany: [231:*27, 28, 39–40*]. NB. These are for the territory of the 1871 *Reich*.
2. Economic development measures (cols 4–5)
   [230:*51ff*].
3. Measure of level of industrialisation (cols 6–8)
   15:*190*].
4. Coal and steel output figures (cols 9–10)
   Measures are in '000s of metric tons.
   Coal figures for Austria, France, Russia and the UK: [230: *188–9*].
   Coal figures for Prussia: [231: *64*].
   Steel figures: [230: *223*]. Note that the Prussian figures are for the territory of the 1871 *Reich*. Prussia produced perhaps 90% of that amount.
5. Levels of central government expenditure (cols 11–12)
   [14: *373*]
6. Military manpower figures [cols 13–15] [15: *197*].
7. Government expenditure on military (cols 16–17)
   [14: *366–7*].
8. Per capita GNP [cols 18–20] [15: *220*].

133

Table II: Some detailed comparisons of Austria, France and Prussia: sources used

1. Military
   [234, 1: *251*].
2. Education
   Austria and France: [235: *table JI*].
   Prussia: [231: *224–5*].
3. Railways
   [233: *792–3*].

Glossary

Deutsche Bund

The translation of this term is German Confederation. This was set up at the Congress of Vienna in June 1815. It consisted of some 39 states ranging from the two major powers of Austria and Prussia to some tiny territorial states in central Germany as well as four city-states. Only the western half of Austria-Hungary (excluding the Italian possessions of Lombardy and Venetia) was included. The Prussian provinces of East and West Prussia as well as the Grand Duchy of Posen were also outside the territory of the Confederation. Some areas within the Confederation were ruled by princes whose major territory was outside. For example, the Duchies of Schleswig and Holstein were ruled by the King of Denmark.

The affairs of the *Bund* were managed by an assembly of state delegates or ambassadors known as the *Bundestag*. This met in permanent session in Frankfurt am Main. Voting was roughly related to the size of member states. Technically individual states were sovereign: this was a confederation not a federation. However, smaller states found it difficult to resist *Bund* decisions which were agreed to by a majority, including Austria and Prussia.

The *Bund* was temporarily out of action during the period of the 1848 revolutions. It was formally restored in 1851. It ceased to exist with the outbreak of the Austro-Prussian war in 1866.

Deutsche Zollverein

The term means German tariff union and refers to an arrangement whereby a number of German states agreed to abolish tariff barriers between themselves and to operate a set of common tariffs externally. There had been various and rival such agreements between different German states in the 1820s. In 1834 Prussia took the lead in establishing what came to be known as the *Deutsche Zollverein* or simply *Zollverein*. At first it consisted of the states of Prussia, the two Hesses, Bavaria, Württemberg, Saxony and some very small central German states. It took on new members as follows: Baden and Nassau (1835); Frankfurt (1836), Brunswick (1841),

135

Hannover (1851), Oldenburg (1852), Schleswig-Holstein (1866), the Mecklenburg states and Lübeck (1868), Alsace-Lorraine (1871). It also negotiated trade treaties with outside states such as France and Austria although these were usually undertaken by the Prussian government in consultation with other states rather than by an independent institution. In 1868 the *Zollverein* established a parliament which consisted of delegates from the *Reichstag* of the North German Confederation and directly elected delegates from the south German states which were part of the *Zollverein* but not of the North German Confederation. This institution was short-lived and lapsed with the establishment of the Second Empire. The powers of the *Zollverein* were taken over by the imperial government once the 1871 *Reich* was established. However, not every member state of the Reich was in the *Zollverein* from the start. Hamburg and Bremen, for example, only joined the *Zollverein* in 1888.

Kleindeutsch

The term means 'little German'. It is used to describe advocates of a German nation-state which excluded the Austria portion of the *Bund*. It is sometimes equated with a pro-Prussian position. However, some *kleindeutsch* advocates sought to devise methods by which Prussian dominance of such a state would be avoided (e.g. by reforming Prussian institutions or breaking up the Prussian state). Conversely, some Prussian patriots envisaged Prussia defeating Austria in war and incorporating Austrian Germans into a Prussian-dominated German state.

Großdeutsch

The term means 'great(er) German'. It is used to describe advocates of a German nation-state which included the Austrian portion of the *Bund*. It is sometimes equated with a pro-Austrian position. However, some *großdeutsch* advocates sought to devise methods by which neither Austria nor Prussia would dominate such a state (e.g. through various democratic and federalist provisions). Some *großdeutsch* advocates were motivated by anti-Prussian rather than pro-Austrian sentiments. Finally, some Austrian patriots envisaged a much larger multinational political creation in central Europe rather than a 'greater Germany' which would involve breaking up the Habsburg Empire.

The term is not to be confused with 'pan-German' or 'greater German' positions developed after 1871. Pan-Germans advocated the attachment of Austrian Germany to the 1871 *Reich*. However, these positions presupposed the dominance of Berlin in such arrangements.

136

Großpreußisch

The term means 'great(er) Prussian'. It is used by historians to describe advocates of Prussian territorial expansion. Bismarck, for example, took up a *großpreußisch* position on the eve of the 1866 war, pointing out to William that all his predecessors had expanded the territory of the Prussian state. The major territorial transformation of 1867 can be described as *großpreußisch* in that it involved such expansion with the annexation by Prussia of Hannover, Schleswig-Holstein, Hesse and Nassau.

The relationship between *großpreußisch* and *kleindeutsch* positions is a complex and changing one.

Mitteleuropa

The term means 'middle (or central) Europe'. It is used by historians of this period to describe those who advocated much tighter relationships between the German states and the rest of the territory of the Habsburg Empire. This was usually not envisaged in terms of a single, sovereign state but rather in terms of either an enlarged *Zollverein* or a *Bund*.

The term is not to be confused with those who, after 1871, advocated a policy of German hegemony – formally or informally – in central Europe.

Chronology

1803	France dictates a major territorial reorganisation of the western half of the Holy Roman Empire by which she gains the left bank of the Rhine and the larger German states receive compensation on the right bank, resulting in the destruction of many small states.
1804	Francis II, Holy Roman Emperor, assumes title of Francis I, Emperor of Austria.
1805	Bavaria and Württemberg raised to status of kingdoms. 3rd war of coalition (including Austria, Britain and Russia) against France. French victories over Russia and Austria. French naval defeat at Trafalgar. Peace of Pressburg: Austrian territorial losses.
1806	End of Holy Roman Empire. Napoleon establishes the Confederation of the Rhine. 4th war of coalition pits Prussia, Russia and Britain against France. French victories over Prussia. Napoleon initiates continental blockade of Britain.
1807	Peace of Tilsit between France and Russia ends war. Prussia reduced to rump state; her lost territory used to form Grand Duchy of Warsaw and Kingdom of Westphalia. Stein appointed first minister in Prussia and begins process of reforms.
1809	5th war of coalition (Austria and Britain against France). Austrian defeat leads to further territorial losses.
1810	Napoleon marries daughter of Austrian Emperor.
1811	Prussia joins in military alliance with France.
1812	Napoleon invades Russia. Retreat begins October. Prussian army signs agreement with Russian army in December.
1813	Prussia declares war on France in March; Austria declares war on France in August. October: France defeated in battle at Leipzig.
1814	Allies enter Paris; May: first Peace of Paris. Peace Congress convened in Vienna agrees territorial settlement of German lands.
1815	Napoleon escapes; defeated at Waterloo. Final Act of Congress of Vienna. German Confederation established. Otto von Bismarck born.

1817	German Student Association (*Burschenschaften*) organise nationalist festival at Wartburg.
1818	Constitutions granted in Baden and Bavaria.
1819	Carlsbad decrees enforce political restrictions on the German states.
1820	Vienna 'Final Act' establishes greater control of Confederation over affairs of individual states.
1823	Provincial Diets established in Prussia.
1830–1	Revolts in Hesse, Brunswick and Saxony lead to granting of constitutions.
1832	Nationalist festival in Hambach.
1833	*Zollverein* agreed; comes into operation in following year.
1837	Hannoverian constitution of 1833 suspended by new king.
1840	Frederick William IV becomes King of Prussia.
1847	Meeting of the Prussian United Diet in Berlin.
1848	Outbreak of revolution in the German lands, other territories of the Habsburg Empire and elsewhere. German National Assembly convenes in Frankfurt in May. Prussia goes to war with Denmark over issue of Schleswig-Holstein. Franz Joseph becomes Emperor of Austria.
1849	Frederick William IV rejects offer of hereditary emperorship of Germany under terms of constitution drawn up by German National Assembly. Counter-revolution, including use of Prussian and other troops against rebels in smaller states, Habsburg troops in Italy and Hungary, and Russian troops in Hungary, carried through.
1850	March: Frederick William IV summons a German Parliament to Erfurt. July: peace agreed between Prussia and Denmark. November: Prussia backs down over Hesse-Cassel, abandons its 'Erfurt Union' plan and agrees to accept authority of Confederation. December: Austrian Chancellor, Schwarzenberg, abandons plan to include all of Habsburg Empire in Confederation.
1851	Confederation formally restored; Bismarck appointed first Prussian ambassador to Federal Diet.
1853	*Zollverein* renewed for further 12 years. Austria unable to form Austro-German customs union and has to settle for commercial treaty with *Zollverein*.
1854–6	Crimean war. Austria neutral but anti-Russian.
1858	Agreement between France and Piedmont to act against Austria. William appointed Regent in Prussia.
1859	War of France and Piedmont against Austria. Austria cedes Lombardy to Piedmont; Piedmont later cedes Savoy and Nice to France. The German National Association (*National Verein*)

139

established. Bismarck appointed Prussian ambassador to Russia.

1860   Prussian Minister of War, Albert von Roon, introduces military reforms into Prussian parliament.

1861   Death of Frederick William IV; William becomes King of Prussia.

1862   Bismarck recalled from his recent appointment as Prussian ambassador to France and appointed Minister-President in midst of constitutional conflict.

1863   Denmarck incorporates Schleswig; German Diet votes for action against Denmark; Hannoverian and Saxon troops enter Holstein.

1864   War of Austria and Prussia against Denmark. By Treaty of Vienna (October) Denmark cedes Schleswig and Holstein to Austria and Prussia.

1865   Convention of Gastein: Austria and Prussia occupy and administer Holstein and Schleswig respectively.

1866   January: renewal of *Zollverein* on low tariff basis which ensures continued exclusion of Austria-Hungary. War of Italy and Prussia against Austria. By Treaty of Prague (August) Austria agrees to her exclusion from Germany and by Treaty of Vienna (October) cedes Venetia to Italy. Prussia annexes Schleswig-Holstein, Hannover, Hesse-Cassel and Frankfurt. The North German Confederation established.

1867   Constitution agreed for North German Confederation, including a lower house (*Reichstag*) elected by universal manhood suffrage. Custom agreement between Confederation and the south German states.

1868   Establishment of a Customs Parliament.

1870–1   War of Prussia and other German states against France.

1871   January: German Second Empire proclaimed at Versailles – William becomes first German Emperor and Bismarck appointed German Chancellor; March: France accepts defeat; May: Treaty of Frankfurt by which France cedes Alsace and Lorraine to Germany and agrees to pay a large war indemnity.

Index

Page references followed by an asterisk refer to definitions in the Glossary

Hall, Carl Christian, 60
Hamburg, 30, 73
Hannover, 23, 30, 31–2, 37, 72,
  73, 75, 90
Hannover, King of, 18, 86
Hapsburg Empire, 7, 15, 23, 41,
  43, 77, 87, 102, 105
Hesse, Elector of, 86
Hessian states, 37, 72, 73, 75, 90
Heydt, von der, 17
Hohenzollern, 30, 77, 89
Hohenzollern, Prince Anton, 94
Holstein, 58, 60, 62, 63, 64, 65,
  72, 74, 90
Holy Roman Empire, 7, 29, 30, 31
Hungary, 40, 43, 65, 78, 89

imperial overstretch, 43
Indemnity Bill, 83, 84–5
industrial capitalism, 9–10
Italy: foundation of kingdom, 20;
  agreement with Prussia, 70–1;
  threat to Austria, 69–70;
  unification, 69; war with Austria,
  79; control of Rome, 88

Kehr, Eckart, 9
Keynes, John Maynard, 6
kleindeutsch, 10, 11, 25, 28, 33,
  62, 71, 136*
kleindeutsch historians, 5
Königgrätz, battle of, 79, 87;
  see also Sadowa
Kossuth, Lajos, 17

Landtag, 50–1, 83
language criteria, 101
Leiningen, Prince, 17
Leipzig, battle of, 21, 79
Leopold, Prince, 89–90
liberal critics of the Reich, 9
liberal German opinion, 15, 90
liberal ideals, 14
Liebknecht, Wilhelm, 8
List, Friedrich, 23
Listz, Franz, 27
Lombardy, 38, 44
London, Treaty of, 58, 59, 62,
  63, 66

Lorraine, 98
low tariff policy see Zollverein
Lübeck, 30, 73
Ludwig II, King of Bavaria, 98
Luxemburg, 69, 77, 88, 90

Magenta, battle of, 21
Magyars, 40, 44, 46, 89
March Charter, 59
Marx, Karl, 3, 101
Mazzini, Giuseppe, 17
Mecklenburg, 73
Metternich, Prince Clemens Lothar,
  29, 43, 45, 105, 112
Metz, 96
middle class, 29
military strength, 13
Miquel, Johannes, 90
Mitteleuropa, 7, 137*
mobilisation: 1866, 71, 75–6, 79;
  1870, 96
Moltke, Helmuth, Count von, 42,
  61, 77, 79–80, 81, 97
Monumenta Germania Historica, 27
Moravia, 38

Napoleon Bonaparte, 29, 52, 112
Napoleon III, Charles Louis:
  opportunist policy, 20, 60,
  68–9; supports Prussian-Italian
  agreement, 70; intrigues, 85;
  misled by Bismark, 77; aims,
  88, 107
Napoleonic changes, 18, 22, 29
Napoleonic occupation, 25
Nassau, 90
Nassau, Duke of, 86
national culture, 24, 91, 106–7
National Liberal Party, 90–1, 93,
  99, 110
national literature, 25
national movements: support for,
  10, 15–17, 106, 108
national symbols, 111, 112
National Verein, 28, 35, 49, 62,
  71–2
nationalism, 8, 10, 98, 112–13
nationalist organisations, 25

third Germany, 2, 7, 8
Third *Reich*, 7
trade in Europe, 12–13
Treitschke, Heinrich von, 5, 6, 98
troop movement, 14, 21, 47, 75–6, 79, 81, 96

unification of Germany, 5, 6–8, 10, 98, 100, 102–3, 112–13

Valentin, Veit, 9
Valmy, battle of, 97
Venetia, 46, 65, 69, 70, 74
Vereine, 49
Versailles, 1, 99
Vienna, 40–1, 43, 76, 85, 104
Vienna, Congress of, 18, 30

weapon improvements *see* rifles
Wehler, Hans-Ulrich, 9
Westphalia: province, 30
Westphalia, Kingdom of, 30

Whig-Liberal governments, 15
William I, King of Prussia: liberal aspirations, 35; succeeds, 51; military reforms, 52; boycotts Princes Congress, 37, 45, 57; breaks with Austria, 66, 78; mobilises, 71; intransigence, 56; military aggression, 78, 85, 112; supports Spanish claim, 94; Emperor, 99
Wittelsbach dynasty, 17
Württemberg, 30, 31, 37, 70, 73, 85, 92, 112

Zollparlament, 92
Zollverein, 135–6*; commercial treaties, 23, 92; customs parliament, 92; effects on unity, 24; excludes Austria, 6, 23, 34, 39, 42; Prussian dominance, 32, 36, 46, 48, 104

145